THE
Great
EMERGENCE

ēmersion

Emergent Village resources for communities of faith

An Emergent Manifesto of Hope
edited by Doug Pagitt and Tony Jones

Organic Community
Joseph R. Myers

Signs of Emergence
Kester Brewin

Justice in the Burbs
Will and Lisa Samson

Intuitive Leadership
Tim Keel

www.emersionbooks.com

THE
Great
EMERGENCE

How Christianity
Is Changing and Why

PHYLLIS TICKLE

BakerBooks

a division of Baker Publishing Group
Grand Rapids, Michigan

Published by Baker Books
a division of Baker Publishing Group
P.O. Box 6287, Grand Rapids, MI 49516-6287
www.bakerbooks.com

Second printing, November 2008

Printed in the United States of America

Library of Congress Cataloging-in-Publication Data
Tickle, Phyllis.
    The great emergence : how Christianity is changing and why / Phyllis Tickle.
        p.   cm.
    ISBN 978-0-8010-1313-3 (cloth)
    1. Christianity—21st century. I. Title.
BR121.3.T53 2008
270.8′3—dc22   2008021706

Contents

List of Illustrations 6
Editor's Preface 7
Preface 9

Part 1 The Great Emergence: What Is It? 13

1. Rummage Sales: When the Church Cleans Out Its Attic 19
2. Cable of Meaning: The Loss and Discovery of a Common Story 33

Part 2 The Great Emergence: How Did It Come to Be? 41

3. The Great Reformation: A Prequel to Emergence 43
4. Questions of Re-formation: Darwin, Freud, and the Power of Myth 63
5. The Century of Emergence: Einstein, the Automobile, and the Marginalization of Grandma 77

Part 3 The Great Emergence: Where Is It Going? 119

6. The Gathering Center: And the Many Faces of a Church Emerging 123
7. The Way Ahead: Mapping Fault Lines and Fusions 145

Index 167

Illustrations

The Cable   35

Popes of the Late Fourteenth and Early Fifteenth Centuries   44

The Quadrilateral   126

The Cruciform   128

The Gathering Center   131

The Rose   137

The Surrounding Currents   140

The Bases of Authority (a)   147

The Bases of Authority (b)   148

Editor's Preface

The Great Emergence is an exemplary book for the ēmersion line. Its goal is to generate straightforward and hope-filled messages to communities of Christian faith.

Phyllis Tickle takes us on a journey—a journey into history, into science, into Christian tradition, into faith. And perhaps most importantly, she takes us on a journey into a faithful future.

For some, this book will serve as an anchor point of understanding how Christianity fits into the large, sweeping scheme of history. For others, it will serve as a new set of lenses to view anew the very experiences of their own passions and frustrations. For still others, it will generate fresh possibilities for the future. But no reader will be left to wonder about the importance of the great emergence on society, faith, and religion.

While Phyllis tells this story, which she does with amazing brevity, humor, and passion, she also inspires the reader to become a participant in the Great Emergence of our day. She serves as a "wise sage" as well as a prophet calling communities of faith to greater levels of participation in what God is about in the world.

The ēmersion line is proud to present this premier contribution, *The Great Emergence.*

Doug Pagitt
General Editor,
emersion: Emergent Village resources
      for communities of faith

Preface

A word or two of explanation seems warranted, since what you are about to read has had a somewhat unusual story behind its presentation here.

While I began life as a teacher—first of Latin to high school students, then as a college instructor, and finally as a college dean—I have spent the bulk of my professional career in publishing. I left the academic world in 1971, in fact, to open and run a small Southern publishing house that, over the years, grew and morphed and grew again. All through those years, however, my yearning and urgency were toward my own writing; and in 1990 I left secular publishing to turn my full attention to living the life of the professional writer. But the late eighties and early nineties were also the years when religion was overtaking every other segment of America's book publishing industry. By 1992, religion as a category of publishing was approaching triple-digit annual growth, and something had to be done by the larger industry to accommodate such massive change.

Publishers Weekly is the trade journal of the book publishing industry in the English language; but prior to 1992, it had not had a religion department for, truth be told, none had been needed. When the tsunami came that year, however, the journal had no choice other than to establish such a department, and quickly. Happily, for me anyway, I knew publishing from years of experience in the industry, I was a devout and observant member of the world's largest religion, and I was free, more or less.

When *Publishers Weekly* called, I was startled at first. Most people who think they have the rest of their lives mapped out, only to discover otherwise, are startled, I suppose. But in due time and after further conversation, I was intrigued, came out of my self-imposed retirement-to-write stance, and went to New York to create out of whole cloth something that had never been before, and do it immediately. My training in religion is, as a result, not in any way formal. Rather, I became a student of religion by being cast dead center of the maelstrom and having to learn to swim right there and right then.

For religion books to get to the general readers who were ravenous for them, religion publishers had to be merged into secular media and secular retail book outlets. The industry's trade journal was the logical forum for the transfer of the data and information required to effect such an integration of the niche into the general market. Many secular publishing houses, for their part, had never done much, if any, religion publishing. Suddenly, however, they had to have effective, accessible, and deadly accurate information about what was happening in American religion, why it was happening, what to publish that would feed the needs thus identified, and what was likely to come next. Again, the industry's journal was the immediately obvious place for that transfer of data.

Over the years of that exchange, I changed too, of course. I became what is called a public intellectual or, in my old haunts as an academic, would have been called "a scholar without portfolio." What those terms mean is that I was in a field where there were not yet programs for formal training. I was, to use the more common

expression, receiving on-the-job training in spades. I was being trans-
formed into a sociologist of religion as it is commercially applied; I
was learning to see religion and its patterns as they could be tracked
and validated in sales figures and book subcategories and title/format
flow as well as in more traditional demographic studies. I also (for I
shall always be an academic) began to read and study what scholars
had said, and were saying, about religion both now and in other
times of upheaval and flux. Always, obviously, I read through the
lens of my own professional obligations at *Publishers Weekly* and in
terms of my own industry's stated expectations of what their trade
journal should provide; but I also learned far more than what was
immediately applicable to publishing needs and purposes.

As a Christian, I became increasingly persuaded that what *Publishers Weekly* had taught me or had allowed me to learn had a greater
place in the Christian community at large. Accordingly, I resigned my
post at the journal and began a whole new life of talking to people—
both lay and ordained—around the country about what it is that is
happening to us just now, and why, and to what probable result. The
book you are about to read is, in essence, a hard copy at last of what
those lectures and speeches and interviews have been about.

One of the great joys for me in writing this book has, in fact,
been the realization that at last I am being given the opportunity
to assemble into one coherent, narrative whole what I have been
delivering in pieces and parts for the last several years. I am grateful
for that gift, just as I shall remain always grateful to those of you who
come to share with me here this particular overview of the Great
Emergence through which we are presently living.

Phyllis Tickle

PART I

THE
Great
EMERGENCE

What Is It?

"The Great Emergence" refers to a monumental phenomenon in our world, and this book asks three questions about it. Or looked at the other way around, this book is about a monumental phenomenon considered from the perspective of three very basic questions: What is this thing? How did it come to be? Where is it going? The third question is loaded, by the way. Fully stated, what it really means to ask is, not just where is this thing going, but also where is it taking us as it goes?

As a phenomenon, the Great Emergence has been slipping up on us for decades in very much the same way spring slips up on us week by week every year. Though it may have sent us a thousand harbingers of its approach, we are still surprised to wake up one balmy morning to a busy, chirping world that, a mere twenty-four hours before, had been a gray and silent one. Our surprise does not mean that all of us have failed to notice the first, subtle shiftings of the seasons. It just means that most of us haven't bothered to think about them; because at a practical or useful level, spring isn't "here" until it's fully enough here to make a difference in our mundane lives—in what we decide to wear, how we plan our activities, and what to do with our time, even in what and how much we decide to eat. So it has been with us and the Great Emergence. If it was indeed coming our way, then most of us would prefer to deal with it after it was fully here and not while it was merely sending intimations of itself.

There has been a certain economy of effort in that "Wait 'til it actually gets here" attitude. For one thing, even during the closing years of the twentieth century, the Great Emergence was as hard to catch as spilled mercury on a high school lab counter. Like mercury, its major, public use was for making either conversation or amateur temperature gauges. For another thing, and very unlike liquid mercury, it was amorphous, lacking any cohesion or, for that matter, any clear borders or definable circumference. But since then, a century has rolled over us, bringing with it the rejuvenating hopes and promises of a new millennium and the keen awareness that, whatever it may be for good or ill, the Great Emergence is to be a major part of this new season in our human years.

Like every "new season," this one we recognize as the Great Emergence affects every part of our lives. In its totality, it interfaces with, and is the context for, everything we do socially, culturally, intellectually, politically, economically. When, for instance, a book on global economics can become a mega-seller, what we are really acknowledging to ourselves at a popular level is something we had already sensed but had not wanted to acknowledge, namely that the world really has gone flat again. Among other things, we are admitting at last that classic economics do not apply nearly so well to a service-based economy as they once did to our production-based ones. We are acknowledging as well that national borders and national loyalties no longer hold as once they did. We are accepting as well the absolute fact that now even a small nation can hold a large one hostage, because technology and the knowledge of how to use it have leveled the playing field. No one is privileged anymore, or at least not in the old ways of physical wealth and sheer manpower.

When we become agitated—and agitate each other—about how we are drowning in information overload, in correspondence, and in the stress of unending "To-Do" lists, we are talking about the Great Emergence, or at least about one small part of its presence as a new time in human history. When, for example, we discover we can no longer do so simple a thing as running sums in our heads, but instead have to turn to our calculators, we are recognizing that we are storing more and more of our "selves" outside of ourselves and thereby creating a dependency that is, at the very least, unsettling. Dependency on machines, in other words, is part of the Great Emergence, and it infiltrates far more than our mundane activities. It infiltrates as well our unsettled and unsettling inability to determine where the line is between us and machines . . . how many of them we will allow into our bodies, how much we will allow them to simulate our actions, how long we will be able to control them. For that matter, we pale before the questions of creating life itself or even of simply engineering it. We grow ever more alarmed that the so-called footprint of human presence in our tech-driven world is killing the earth, yet we feel powerless to stop her demise. Or we have to accept the relativeness of universal laws and the unpredictabilities of quantum physics and cannot stop those facts from leeching over into our ways of seeing "truth" and "fact." These also are signs and evidences of the Great Emergence. Their listing, in fact, is almost boundless, so pervasive is the nature of the shift we are passing through.

It is, however, not with the whole of the Great Emergence that we are concerned here. Rather, it is with religion—and specifically with Christianity in North America—that we are concerned at the moment.

The Right Reverend Mark Dyer, an Anglican bishop known for his wit as well as his wisdom, famously observes from time to time that the only way to understand what is currently happening to us as twenty-first-century Christians in North America is first to understand that about every five hundred years the Church feels compelled to hold a giant rummage sale. And, he goes on to say, we are living in and through one of those five-hundred-year sales. Now, while the bishop may be using a bit of humor to make a point, his is nonetheless a deadly serious and exquisitely accurate point. Any usable discussion of the Great Emergence and what is happening in Christianity today must commence with yesterday and a discussion of history. Only history can expose the patterns and confluences of the past in such a way as to help us identify the patterns and flow of our own times and occupy them more faithfully.

The first pattern that we must consider as relevant to the Great Emergence is Bishop Dyer's rummage sale, which, as a pattern, is not only foundational to our understanding but also psychologically very reassuring for most of us. That is, as Bishop Dyer observes, about every five hundred years the empowered structures of institutionalized Christianity, whatever they may be at that time, become an intolerable carapace that must be shattered in order that renewal and new growth may occur. When that mighty upheaval happens, history shows us, there are always at least three consistent results or corollary events.

First, a new, more vital form of Christianity does indeed emerge. Second, the organized expression of Christianity which up until then had been the dominant one is reconstituted into a more pure and less ossified expression of its former self. As a result of this usually energetic but rarely benign process, the Church actually ends up with two new creatures where once there had been only one. That is, in the course of birthing a brand-new expression of its faith and praxis, the Church also gains a grand refurbishment of the older one. The third result is of equal, if not greater, significance, though. That is, every time the incrustations of an overly established Christianity have been broken open, the faith has spread—and been spread— dramatically into new geographic and demographic areas, thereby increasing exponentially the range and depth of Christianity's reach as a result of its time of unease and distress. Thus, for example, the birth of Protestantism not only established a new, powerful way of being Christian, but it also forced Roman Catholicism to make changes in its own structures and praxis. As a result of both those changes, Christianity was spread over far more of the earth's territories than had ever been true in the past.

1

Rummage Sales

When the Church Cleans Out Its Attic

Five hundred years back from our twenty-first century places us solidly in the sixteenth century and what is now being called "The Great Reformation." The *Great* part in that term, while it has always been there to some extent, was not much used in general conversation until fairly recently. One of the amusing, though hardly major, details of current religious discussion, in fact, is how *Great* as a qualifier has come to insinuate itself into popular discussions of the Reformation. We human beings discover what we know by listening to ourselves talk; and the installation of *Great* as a permanent part of "The Great Reformation" speaks volumes about our unselfconscious awareness of a pattern that more folk than just bishops are beginning to engage.

If then, five hundred years back from our time takes us to the Great Reformation, where does five hundred years back from the Great Reformation take us? Obviously to the Great Schism, which happily has had its *Great* all along and for good reason.

Most of us have some working knowledge of the sixteenth century. If we don't know in detail what Martin Luther thought and wrote, we do know who he was and that we live in the consequences of whatever it was that he did think and write. We are aware in general, if not in particular, that there were other men like Luther—men like Wycliffe and Müntzer and Zwingli, Knox and Calvin and Hooker—who also were discomforted with the Roman Church, but who disagreed violently among themselves about what to do with their discontent. The result was Protestant Christianity with all its grandeur, its shredding divisiveness, and its inestimable gifts of rationalism and enlightenment upon which Western culture now stands. But not so with the Great Schism.

The Great Schism is for most of us more a faintly familiar combination of words than a sharply defined event in history. In dealing with our times of re-formation, we have a tendency to assign a specific date to them, a particular time to which we can point and say, "Aha! Here is where and when this thing happened." For the Great Reformation, that date is October 31, 1517, and Luther's alleged nailing of his 95 Theses to the door of the church in Wittenberg. For reasons we shall see shortly, the Great Reformation no more began in 1517 than it ended in 1518. Assigning a date to it is more a matter of convenience than of accuracy. A date allows us to feel that we have some grip upon the thing, whether we do or not. And the date for the Great Schism is 1054, a neat and convenient five centuries prior.

Like 1517, 1054 is assigned to the Great Schism because it was the date of a particular and a pivotal event. Luther had his Theses and his hammer. In 1054, the Patriarch of Greek or Eastern Orthodox Christianity had his anathemas and Leo IX had his bulls of excommunication. The Patriarch had Constantinople and the Pope had Rome. One had Greek and used leavened bread for the mass and believed that the Holy Spirit descended from God the Father. The other called Latin the language of God and God's uses, used only unleavened bread in the communion meal, and argued that the Holy Spirit descends equally from God the Father and God the Son.

While questions about whose mother tongue is to be used in worship and about whether or not yeast should be incorporated in consecrated bread may seem minor to us now, they were not in the eleventh century. They were major, not just because of religious enthusiasms, but because of what they symbolized in each of the cultures for which they were habit and sacred means. As we shall see over and over again, religious enthusiasms in all holy rummage sales are unfailingly symptomatic or expressive of concomitant political, economic, and social upheavals. And in the year 1054, all those pieces and parts of two rapidly diverging cultures that had coexisted in a state of discontent and unrest with each other for more than a century coalesced at last over the *filioque*, or in plain English, over where, how, and from whom the Holy Spirit comes. Rome excommunicated Constantinople, and Constantinople, which saw itself as Constantine's creation of a better, purer Rome, returned the compliment. It would be a Crusade or two and a millennium later before the breach would be repaired. Greek and/or Eastern Orthodoxy would be the faith of the Eastern world, and Roman Catholicism would be the dominant expression of Christianity in the West.

Gregory the Great

Five hundred years prior to the Great Schism takes us to the sixth century and what once upon a very recent time was labeled as "The Fall of the Roman Empire" or "The Coming of the Dark Ages." Nowadays, however, some wits are increasingly pleased to say that going back five hundred years from the Great Schism takes us to Gregory the Great. While this is a joke or tongue-in-cheek acknowledgment of over many *great*'s among us, it nonetheless is arguably accurate. For one thing, Gregory, who technically is Gregory I in terms of papal ascent and St. Gregory I in the Roman tradition, has been popularly referred to as Gregory the Great almost from the beginning, and for very good reason.

Born ca. 540 CE, Gregory came to the papacy sometime around 590 CE, which means that he did indeed preside over the closing decade of the tumultuous sixth century and the first four years of the new century. Far more important, however, and unique to this re-formation is the fact that Gregory I did not become Gregory the Great because of what he did to lead a revolution. He became "the Great" because of his brilliance in cleaning one up. Popular or lay recognition of Gregory's greatness—he was canonized immediately after his death in response to public demand, in fact—rests, instead, upon his having led a continent that was in total upheaval into some kind of ecclesio-political coherence and, building on the work of St. Benedict, upon his having guided Christianity firmly into the monasticism that would protect, preserve, and characterize it during the next five centuries.

As we shall see in greater detail later, each of the five-hundred-year re-formations that we have gone through as a people has had many contributing factors, many events that came into confluence and tripped every aspect of communal life over into chaos. The upheaval of the sixth century was, however, the most chaotic of them all and the one to which it is most difficult to assign a single date. It is impossible, in this instance, to say of a single person, "Ahhh! Here was the leader of this thing," or of an event, "Here—just here—is where it really became obvious that reformation was in process."

Rome was, by the sixth century, dead. It had been dying for quite a long time, but moribund and dead are not exactly the same thing. In 410 CE the barbarian hordes successfully breached the city's walls for the first time. They would return after that, time and time again; but it was not until 480 CE that the Roman Senate finally and officially disbanded itself in recognition of the fact that there was no longer either a city or an empire to govern. In between those two pivotal dates, there is another, equally informing one for Christianity.

In 451, in the city of Chalcedon in Asia Minor, the Eastern emperor Marcian convened the Church's Fourth Ecumenical Council, known now, unimaginatively enough, as the Council of Chalcedon. Marcian was a devout Christian as well as a skilled politician. Functioning out of both those skill sets, he assembled the Council in order to determine, and then codify, what was, and was not, correct doctrine. Several elements of two basic issues were threatening to break the Church apart, and especially to sever the bonds of commonality and affection between Western Christianity and some parts of African and Middle-Eastern Christianity. Those major questions were whether or not Mary could be called "Mother of God" and whether or not Jesus was one "person" of two natures or two "persons" inside one skin. Like yeast in communion bread, it's a bit hard for us today to grasp the seriousness of such differences, much less to empathize with the passion which surrounded them. What really was at stake, of course, was the nature of incarnation, that is, the nature of what Jesus of Nazareth was. By calling Mary "the Mother of God," we imply that His divinity and His physicality are inseparable, that He was indeed "one Person in two natures." And by saying "one Person in two natures," we obviously are asserting that God and humanity were totally and inviolately integrated in Jesus of Nazareth and that He is of the same substance as both the Father and us.

Not only is it difficult for many twenty-first-century Christians to fathom the ferocity of the Chalcedonian arguments, but it has also been even more difficult at times for Protestants to appreciate the full implications of why "Mother of God" historically should matter as much to them as it does to Roman Catholic Christians. If Protestantism does not venerate the Virgin, it still owes to the Roman insistence on doing so an appreciation of what might otherwise have been the Western Christian traditions out of which Protestantism came. Had Chalcedon accepted Mary only as mother of the human vessel in which the divine was trapped or out of which it operated—had it, in other words, rejected the Virgin as "Mother of God" and discerned instead two entities, only one of which she was the mother of—Christian doctrine would have been open to conceptualizing Jesus as a guru soul inhabiting for a time a human vessel. Even the agony of the cross itself and of the path leading to it would have thereby been diminished and rendered less sacrificial.

But not everybody at the Council of Chalcedon was of one mind or spirit after the battles were, technically speaking, "over." So bitter was the dissension and so vociferous were the arguments, in fact, that in the end Oriental Christianity was exiled from (or withdrew from, depending on one's point of view) both Western and Eastern Christianity. Chalcedon was, that is, the beginning of what are still today the three grand divisions of the faith: Western Christianity, which at the opening of the twentieth century was composed largely by Roman Catholicism and Protestantism; Eastern Orthodoxy (also often called Greek Orthodoxy), which traditionally is thought of as existing primarily in Greece, Asia Minor, Eastern Europe, and Russia, but today has a firm and increasingly secure footing in North America, China, Finland, and Japan; and Oriental Orthodoxy (or the Oriental Orthodox Church, again depending on one's point of view), which in our time is also growing in strength and is usually subtitled as Coptic, Ethiopian, Armenian, or Syrian Christianity.

How Gregory and the Monastics Saved Civilization

Stupendous as this reconfiguration was, and has been, for global Christianity in all three of its major parts, the agonies of the sixth century gave something of far more immediate and dramatic use to Western Christianity and culture. They gave the Western world a reconfigured form of monasticism that functioned not only as a way of private holiness but also as a way of societal and political stability.

During the long decline of its civil governance, the population of Rome was increasingly composed of illiterate barbarians who had grown weary of raiding the Eternal City and decided instead to take up residency and stay awhile. Because Christianity was the religion of the Empire, many, many of these new raiders-turned-citizens adopted it; but they also and inevitably adapted it as well.

The holy writings of the new Christian canon, the sayings and teachings of the Desert Fathers, the liturgy of the urban basilicas, the homilies of the great men of the Early Church, the observance of the daily prayers—all these things that are familiar to us now and that had been the Christianity of Constantine and his immediate successors require at least a rudimentary literacy as well as a civil stability that allows the free flow of worshipers from home or business to places of worship and godly instruction. Late fifth-century Romans had neither. Instead, they had a growing illiteracy in their domestic worship and unmanageable lawlessness in their streets. What politically and culturally would very swiftly spiral down into the Dark Ages was already at work peeling the Christianity of the Early Church away from the laity and inserting into the resulting vacuum a kind of animistic, half-magical form of a bastardized Christianity that would characterize the laity and much of the minor clergy over the next few centuries.

During those centuries of darkness, and largely because of Gregory's prescience and acumen, Western Christianity would be held in trust in Europe's convents and monasteries. The monks and nuns would not all be pure or brilliant or even, in many cases, themselves literate. But enough of them would be so that the great treasures of the first five centuries of the Church would be preserved, and then added to, by the great minds of the Dark Ages. Almost all of those conservators and pioneering thinkers were Christian clergy, monks, or nuns; all of them were educated either in monasteries and convents or as a result of them. And that sanctuary for both the exercise of the Christian faith and the perpetuation of intellectual vigor and excellence was the direct product of one St. Gregory I who laid the foundation upon which it rested. Before it was all over, Europe would discover that such power as there was in that fearsome time was the power of the abbots and the abbesses, the priors and the prioresses.

The tumultuous reconfigurations of the sixth century, pivotal as they were for the faith, pale in importance before those of the first century. It is here, of course, that Christianity is born. The birth, public ministry, teachings, crucifixion, and resurrection of Jesus of Nazareth as Messiah would cause even the epochs of human time to be redated, and this by believers and nonbelievers alike. In that momentous century, the Judaism out of which the new faith came and Messiah spoke was ground down into such small parts that its adherents would be forced to leave their natal land, regroup, and ultimately broadcast the seeds of their faith, be it Christian or Jewish, all over the known world. In 70 CE the Temple of stone would be destroyed. In 130 CE the Holy City would be permanently barred against Jewish blood even entering it. And between those two dates, much of the structure that we know as the Church was born.

The Inner Workings of Rummage Sales

When Christians despair of the upheavals and re-formations that have been the history of our faith—when the faithful resist, as so many do just now, the presence of another time of reconfiguration with its inevitable pain—we all would do well to remember that, not only are we in the hinge of a five-hundred-year period, but we are also the direct product of one. We need, as well, to gauge our pain against the patterns and gains of each of the previous hinge times through which we have already passed. It is especially important to remember that no standing form of organized Christian faith has ever been destroyed by one of our semi-millennial eruptions. Instead, each simply has lost hegemony or pride of place to the new and not-yet-organized form that was birthing.

During the sixth century, the Apostolic Church, with its presbyters and anchorites, gave way to an organized monasticism as the true keeper and promulgator of the faith. Yet we must remember three things: first, the Apostolic tradition, with its canon, its John Cassians, and its Augustinian theology, even its pursuit of mysticism, did not cease to be. Second, because of the reconfiguration of those treasures into new shapes and vessels and accommodations, the faith they testify to was scattered across a far broader geographic and demographic area than it had previously occupied. And third, Oriental Christianity most certainly did not cease to be. Rather, it was freed to develop a praxis, liturgy, and theological richness that are today of ever more fascination and interest to the rest of the Church.

In sum, what all of this means is that the more organized, formalized monasticism which came with the sixth century never left us either in tradition or by practice. In adapted and updated forms, monasticism still influences and informs Christianity all over the world. All that really happened was that its somewhat decentralized system gave way to an increasingly more centralized one in Rome. Rome in turn, for political as well as religious reasons, severed itself in the eleventh century from a non-Western threat to its absolute theological and ecclesial authority. In that Great Schism, however, Eastern or Orthodox Christianity was hardly destroyed. Far from it. Instead, it was freed to become fully itself and fully an expression of its own experience of living out the Christian faith in its own circumstances. Indeed, one of the great gains of the last half century for North American Christianity has been the re-introduction of Orthodoxy to Western Christian practice, understanding, and appreciation.

Certainly, as is patently obvious, Roman Catholicism did not cease to exist with the coming of Protestantism in the sixteenth century. It did, however, lose dominance, social and political as well as religious. But any honest observer would have to say that in the course of that loss, the Roman Church was itself also freed—freed to weed out its errors and corruptions while at the same time evolving a more "Roman" way of being "Roman" than had previously been the case. That very process, which the scholar Diana Butler Bass calls "re-traditioning," has occurred with each turn of the eras and is a substantial dynamic in the progression from upheaval to renewed stability.[1] It certainly constitutes an important part of what must be discussed in any analysis of where both established Protestant and Emergent Christianity are going—and taking us—in both the near and more distant future. And "taking us," we must remember, is central to any analysis of re-formations, whether past or present.

When an overly institutionalized form of Christianity is, or ever has been, battered into pieces and opened to the air of the world around it, that faith-form has both itself spread and also enabled the spread of the young upstart that afflicted it. Christianity became a global religion as a result of the Great Reformation. A large part of that globalization was in direct consequence of Protestantism's adamant insistence on literacy, which in turn led more or less directly to the technology that enabled world exploration and trade. As a result, Catholics and Protestants alike could, and did, carry Christianity out of Europe and into the world beyond, often in strenuous—and energizing—competition with each other. But the more or less colonialized Church that Reformation Protestantism and Catholicism managed to plant was, obviously, more or less colonialized, with all the demeaning psychological, political, cultural, and social overtones and resentments which that term brings with it. One does not have to be particularly gifted as a seer these days, however, to perceive the Great Emergence already swirling like balm across that wound, bandaging it with genuinely egalitarian conversation and with an undergirding assumption of shared brotherhood and sisterhood in a world being redeemed.

Broader Upheaval

Before we entirely leave the discussion of rummage sales, though, one or two further points should be made just in the interest of thoroughness, if nothing else. While this present discussion is concerned more or less entirely with Christianity and with our perceptions as North American observers of a mighty upheaval, we still need to acknowledge the existence of rummage sales elsewhere and among other faiths. Specifically, when a Christian speaker talks to a Jewish audience about five-hundred-year cycles, almost always some good rabbi will point out that much the same sort of scheme appertains to Judaism. That is, if one goes back five hundred years from the destruction of the Second Temple and priestly Judaism in the first century CE, one hits the Babylonian Captivity which decimated Solomon's Temple and scattered Judaism away from Judea and into much of the Middle Eastern world. Five hundred years before the Captivity, our good rabbi will point out, was the end of the Age of the Judges and the establishment of the monarchy out of which King David and the Davidic line would come in preparation for Messiah. Thus it can be legitimately argued that what we have in our cycling ways is not so much a Christian phenomenon or pattern as it is a Judeo-Christian one. Of late, an Islamic scholar or two has begun to argue that the same kind of cycling can be discerned in that faith's history. If that can be true, we may be able in time to say that ours is but one presentation of an even larger pattern that informs all three of the faiths of Abraham.

We should also note, if only in passing, that Christianity's pattern of cycling may be seen as peculiar not only to itself and to either or both of its religious siblings but also to something more general. That is, there is a more or less definable period in history that stretches from ca. 900 BCE to ca. 200 BCE, which, if one chooses to see it that way, incorporates two upheavals under one name. The shorthand of one label may be due to the fact that our distance from the immediacy of those centuries allows us the emotional and cultural remove to lump them together into one. Whatever the reasons for their grouping, though, the centuries from 900 to 200 BCE have long been recognized by even armchair historians as seminal for human civilization. Not only did David and Elijah and Jeremiah live during this time, but so too did Socrates, Plato, and Aristotle, not to mention Confucius or the souls that wrote down the *Upanishads* and sang the *Bhagavad-Gita*, or Lord Mahavira, Siddhartha, the Buddha, and Homer with his epic record of Zeus and his fellow gods. This time, it was humanity, in other words, that was emerging; and it was bringing with it both its religions and a growing sense of itself as more than victim to circumstance.

It was not, however, until 1948 that a name was assigned to those centuries of tumultuous transition. In that year, a German scholar, Karl Jaspers, applied the name "the Axial Age" to it; and the name stuck until 2006. In 2006, Karen Armstrong, a scholar of great distinction but also of broad, popular appeal, produced a brilliantly researched and highly influential treatment of the Axial and pre-

Axial centuries under the title of *The Great Transformation*.[2] Her term seems to have stuck, thereby adding yet another *great* to our catalog description of rummage sales.

---

1. See in particular her *The Practicing Congregation* (Herndon, VA: The Alban Institute, 2004) and, with Joseph Stewart-Sicking, her *From Nomads to Pilgrims: Stories from Practicing Congregations* (Herndon, VA: The Alban Institute, 2006).

2. *The Great Transformation: The Beginning of Our Religious Traditions* (New York: Alfred A. Knopf, 2006).

2

Cable of Meaning

The Loss and Discovery of a Common Story

Any careful reader will already have observed that in each of our five-hundred-year hinge times more than religion has been in turmoil. There is a very good reason for that: religion is a social construct. As an assertion so bald-facedly stated, this one is often offensive initially to many people of deep faith. That does not change the truth of the statement. Religion is a social construct as well as an individual or private way of being and understanding.

In its public or corporate role, any established or organized religion is the soul of the culture or society that, in turn, is the body in which and through which religion acts. To go very far into a discussion of the Great Emergence or any other era of re-formation requires us, in other words, to lay aside for a brief while our adherence to a particular faith and consider instead the generic phenomenon of religion as an undifferentiated entity.

A Holy Tether

Looked at as generic rather than personal, religion can be most easily or accessibly described as a kind of cable—a cable of meaning that keeps the human social unit connected to some purpose and/or power greater than itself. Like a little dinghy tethered to a distant dock, the human grouping is secured by that cable. Whether gathered into a tiny, familial grouping of four or five people or into massive ones of tribes and nations, it is always the nature of humanity to turn and ask, "Why?" Life is simply too hard and too painful for us to endure, if endurance is the only purpose. We feel instinctively that there must be more—more reason for our being here, more purpose by which to govern our conduct and inform our choices. More than one philosopher has remarked that if there were no god, we would have to invent one; and the reason is this very thing of existential despair and huge vulnerability.

This does not mean—and even suggest—of course, that all religion is of humanity's making. It does mean, though, that God-given faith assumes group as well as individual shapes and functions, the most obvious of these being its function as the bearer of meaning and its shape or role as a securing connection to something larger than the dinghy.

That cable, like any more ordinary ones, can be opened and its component parts exposed to our view. The thing itself is enclosed in an outer and, so to speak, waterproof casing that keeps the seawater out and the cable's interior in good working order. That waterproof casing we call the *story*. That is, it represents the shared history—mythic, actual, and assumed—of the social unit. It is the ethos, to use a term currently in vogue, that all the members of the unit share, that they hold unself-consciously in common and by which they recognize one another as being alike or of one piece.

Interior to the outer casing of story is a loosely knit, mesh sleeve that, because of its pliable construction, can give and take a bit as the

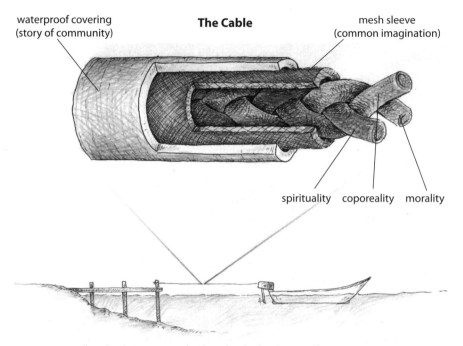

The Cable

waterproof covering
(story of community)

mesh sleeve
(common imagination)

spirituality   coporeality   morality

Illustration by Justin Banger for *The Nick and Josh Podcast*. Used by permission.

little boat rocks along on the waves outside. That sleeve has various names. It is sometimes called the *consensual illusion* and sometimes the *common imagination* and sometimes by combinations of those two. Either way, the mesh sleeve is the common agreement—again often unself-awaredly so—among the members of the social unit about how the world works, about how it is to be imaged and thereby understood. That common and consensual imagining does not have to be factually true at all. It simply has to be the general, operating opinion of the group for whom it serves as both true and actual.

To use a simplistic example, the world was, effectively speaking, flat so long as the majority of our forebears thought it was flat. Its being ovoid was simply not within their illusion or imagining of reality and, therefore, was beyond their engagement. Accordingly, they structured their worldview and their living to accommodate a flat world.

Anatomy of Meaning

Interior to the mesh sleeve of consensual imagination are three strands or lengths of rope braided together into one. The first of these is spirituality. The second is corporeality; and the third, morality.

Of recent years, we have bandied the word *spirituality* about with such abandon that it almost lacks clear definition by now. For our purposes here, however, it is probably sufficient to say that spirituality means to name those experiences and values that are internal to the individual or to the individuals who compose a society.

By the same process, morality can probably be best defined in this situation as the externalization and/or objective enactment and application of the values and experiences of the individual or individuals who compose a society. In between those two bookends is corporeality.

Corporeality is a ten-dollar word for a fairly simple concept. As its etymology suggests, it means to name all the overt, physical— i.e., "embodied"—evidences that a religion exists. In our time and in the case of Christianity, it refers, for instance, to everything from the collar around a priest's neck to the established canon of our Scriptures, from a church building and the debt it carries to a hymnbook and the battle over it, from a doctrinal statement and the battle over that to something so painful as a clerical sex scandal. Diverse as that listing may seem, every part of it is, as required by definition, physical and overt evidence that a religion is in place.[1]

Being so constructed, our cable does its job of securing human life to meaningfulness quite nicely so long as nothing threatens its parts. Sometimes something will come along and prick the outer casing of story and the cable will ship a bit of water; but as a rule, the tear will heal itself in a short time, and all will be well again. Occasionally, the interior mesh sleeve of the common imagination will snag a bit on a piece of the center braid, but the rise and fall of the sea generally works it back into pattern without major incident. And so all is well with the cable until . . .

. . . until that fateful time, about once every five hundred years, when the outer casing of the story and the inner sleeve of the shared illusion take a blow simultaneously. When that happens, a hole is opened straight through to the braid. The water rushes in; and human nature being what human nature is, we reach our collective hand in through the hole and pull out the three strands one at a time. Spirituality first, corporeality second, and morality last. We pull each up, consider it from every possible angle, and at times finger it beyond all imagining. (Consider, for example, how many thousands and thousands of Americans over the last fifty years have been vociferously "spiritual, but not religious.") Once we are satisfied with our understanding of one strand, we stuff it back through the hole and into the braid from which we have lifted it. Then we take on the next strand, worry it to death, in time return it to its former place, and take on the third and last strand.

The Art of Mending

Once we—or the social unit, that is—are done, we always manage to sashay the mesh sleeve back and forth enough to heal the rip in our illusion and by some means—probably more analogous to religious duct tape than to anything else—we manage to reseal the waterproof casing of our story as well. The dinghy is once more secured and its passengers free to turn their attention to matters of fishing or pondering or whatever it is they are about. The interesting thing, for our purposes, though, is that the fishing and pondering are good only for about two hundred and fifty years. That is, the business of winding sufficient duct tape around the casing to make it hold takes us about a century or so, as a rule. It takes that long, because the whole process involves many arguments about how best to do the job, as well as several, usually bloody, encounters with the tools by which we are trying to splice and apply the tape. But at the end of that century or so of contentiousness and just about the time we have settled down into about two hundred and fifty years of thinking that all is at last well and that things are running in their proper order, here comes another century or century and a half in which the casing and the sleeve once more begin to both be bombarded and, eventually, to pock at the same time. To give that third part of the process its more dignified due, we refer to it, of course, not as a time of pocking, but as a peri-reformation. Regardless of the wording, though, the effect is the same, and the cycle has been kick-started all over again.

The Great Emergence is the result of time's most recent kick-start, just as it is in perfect consonance with an apparent cycle in Christian affairs that well may be a cycle in human affairs in general. Having defined where the Great Emergence fits by type or pattern into the greater scheme of history is not enough, however. We want also to understand where it is going and where, in its going, it is taking us. To do that, we must look at the particularities and peculiarities of this re-formation of ours and at how it came to assume its present shape and trajectory. But to look interpretatively and profitably at one's own times with confidence in the result, it is usually wise to look first at the particularities and peculiarities of analogous times. Then, with both the perspective of history and an understanding of the interplay of all the parts of religion firmly in hand, we will be ready to look in some detail at the accumulation of events that birthed, and now sustain and shape, the Great Emergence.

---

1. Corporeality's active presence in religion is also the reason why doctrinal differences like those surrounding homosexuality, for example, are more honestly and effectively dealt with as corporeal rather than as moral issues.

PART 2

THE
Great
EMERGENCE

How Did It Come to Be?

The Great Emergence, whatever else it is or may become, is first and foremost the product of a recurrent pattern in Christian affairs. There is considerable benefit to all of us in exposing the presence of that pattern to public view. For one thing, seeing it allows those of us who are living through the current upheaval to more accurately evaluate and more wisely address the changes that seem at times almost to be swamping our ship. For another—and this often feels more important at a personal level—discovering and exposing pattern can greatly diminish our sense, either corporately or individually, that somehow, "This mess must be our/my fault. It must be because of something we/I did somewhere back along the way." That simply is not true in the grand details, though it may be in some of the more minor, enabling ones. Guilt is neither appropriate, justified, or productive, in other words, when one comes to consider prayerfully and faithfully the Great Emergence. And there is no better way to shed the weight of it than by looking with clear eyes and informed minds at what has got us to this place.

To consider with clear vision and informed minds how the Great Emergence came to be and why it is presenting as it is, we would do well to look first at how some previous re-formation came to be and what general characteristics informed it. By doing so, we will allow ourselves the insights that historical parallels always provide and the comfort, as well, of feeling as if we are less alone, less trapped in some kind of anomaly. For such purposes, a brief overview of the Great Reformation of the sixteenth century is ideal. Not only are we closer in time and culture to the Great Reformation than to any other of the previous hinge times, but also most of us have at least a modicum of knowledge about the history of that era—of the major events and characteristics of its peri-Reformation, Reformation, and post-Reformation periods.

3

The Great Reformation

A Prequel to Emergence

As we know, the Great Reformation no more began on October 31, 1517, than adulthood commences on the morning of one's twenty-first birthday. Both are convenient place markers. Both put a useful handle on a major event that spreads out on either side thereof like a square parcel being carried by a single strap. There's a kind of convenient shorthand involved in that, however. When (and assuming) Martin Luther tacked his theses to the door of the church at Wittenberg Castle, he was responding to pressures that had been building around his natal form of Christianity and culture for over a century. The story and the common imagination of Catholic Europe had been pounded over and over again until they had both pocked at the same time. All Luther did on October 31, 1517, was say, "Look, there's a hole!" followed by the observation, "We're shipping water here, folks."

When the Great Reformation actually began varies in accord with which historian one is reading at the time.[1] There is a kind of consensus, though, that the closing years of the fourteenth century were those in which the die was cast. After 1378, there probably could not have been any turning back. That year was so fraught with disaster, in fact, that it is frequently referred to as "a Great Schism" itself, or sometimes as "the Second Great Schism."

Tensions between the peoples and powers of Italy and princes and powers of France led in 1378 to the simultaneous election of two men to the Chair of Peter: Urban VI, the Italian pope, and Clement VII, the French one. Each ferociously defended his claim to the papal throne while lambasting the other as illegitimate and heretical. Not only did each wage war against the other, but so too did their factions. The resulting chaos was as much cultural, political, and social as it was religious. The primacy of the papacy and the relative unity and stability its authority had formerly exercised in European affairs were both shattered. The phenomenon of two warring popes would not be resolved until 1418. By that time an Italian with the apostolic name of Gregory XII would be contending against a French pope known as Benedict XIII; and both of them would be in contention with another Italian with the apostolic name of John XXIII.

While having three warring popes all claiming to be the one, true Pope may seem somewhere between quaint and downright

Popes of the Late Fourteenth and Early Fifteenth Century

Clement VII	Benedict XIII

Innocent

Gregory XI | Urban VI | Boniface IX | VII Gregory XII | Martin V

Alexander V John XXIII

1378   1388   1398   1408   1418

☐ Avignon   ☐ Rome   ☐ Pisa

ludicrous to us now, it did not seem so to the Church and citizenry of the early fifteenth century. And though they might not have had the perspective from which to analyze their circumstances, we do. The presence of three sitting popes is an almost perfect example of what established forms of religion do during the run up to a hinge time. In the case of the Great Reformation, by contending among themselves, the multiple popes did two, intertwined things. First, they simultaneously pocked both the story and the consensual illusion that has been functional up until 1378. (Up until then, the world of human affairs had run on the principle that there was one Pope and that he was directly and specifically chosen of God to be the final arbitrator, not only of religious matters, but also of political ones. The Christian story asserted this . . . or it always had when it was interpreted to the people by their clergy.) Second, two or three popes evoked the one question that is *always* present in re-formation: Where now is the authority?

Negotiating Authority

Always without fail, the thing that gets lost early in the process of a reconfiguration is any clear and general understanding of who or what is to be used as the arbitrator of correct belief, action, and control. So long as that question remains unanswered, the lens of the common or shared imagination through which we view life in our own time and place is so opaque that we stumble and fall over and over again. The Reformation, when it finally and fully arrived after 1517, was to answer the question almost immediately. *Sola scriptura, scriptura sola.* Only the Scripture and the Scriptures only. Luther and the reformers who followed after him would build their reformed Church on that principle, joining it in good time with the concept of the priesthood of all believers. No more Pope, no more magisterium, no more human confessor between humanity and Christian God, only the Good Book.

The obvious, general benefit of "Scripture only and only Scripture" was that once a new source of unimpeachable authority has been duly constituted and established, things always begin to wind back down from chaos to relative stability again. A more long-range benefit of the Reformation's placing ultimate authority in Scripture was that, when coupled with the principle of the priesthood of all believers, *sola scriptura* required absolute and universal literacy if it were going to work. The Protestant imperative toward every believer's being able to read Holy Writ for him- or herself excited the drive toward literacy that in turn accelerated the drive toward rationalism and from there to Enlightenment and from there straight into the science and technology and literature and governments that characterize our lives today. There were, of course, some disadvantages.

The most obvious problem of universal literacy is that if one teaches five people to read and then asks them each to read the same document, there will be at least three different interpretations of what the five of them have read. While we may laugh and say that divisiveness was Protestantism's greatest gift to Christianity, ours is a somber joke. Denominationalism is a disunity in the body of Christ and, ironically, one that has a bloody history. And there is another irony as well.

Now, some five hundred years later, even many of the most die-hard Protestants among us have grown suspicious of "Scripture and Scripture only." We question what the words mean—literally? Metaphorically? Actually? We even question which words do and do not belong in Scripture and the purity of the editorial line of descent of those that do. We begin to refer to Luther's principle of *"sola scriptura, scriptura sola"* as having been little more than the creation of a paper pope in place of a flesh and blood one. And even as we speak, the authority that has been in place for five hundred years withers away in our hands. "Where now is the authority?" circles overhead like a dark angel goading us toward disestablishment. Where indeed?

The century or so of peri-Reformation running up to Luther and to a fully articulated Reformation was rife with more challenges to the authority of the common illusion and the extant cultural story than just the presence of three warring pretenders to the papacy. Perhaps, in aggregate, the largest number of these assaults was tied directly to Islam and the almost constant warfare between Christian Europe and an Islam that wanted to occupy it. In 1453, the Ottoman Turks finally succeeded in capturing Constantinople with the result that thousands of Greek Orthodox scholars, traders, and intelligentsia fled what is now Turkey to take up residence in Europe. What they carried with them was threefold. First, they brought copies upon copies of the ancient writers who had informed their hereditary culture—Homer, Pythagoras, Plato, Aristotle, the great dramatists, Euclid, Demosthenes, and their kind—along with the great Roman writers—Lucretius, Ovid, Cicero, Pliny, and their kind.

In addition to possessing those codices, the exiled Greeks possessed the ability to read the ancient, classical tongues with sophisticated accuracy. Beyond both those things, however, and arguably of even greater importance in the long reach of history, they brought with them the spectacular scientific and mathematical knowledge of the Arab/Islamic culture in which they had been living. Theirs was, in sum, an accumulated base of pure knowledge that was far in advance of anything medieval Europe had even dreamed of up to that point. And it would be the twentieth century, with its burgeoning sciences, before the West would experience again such an inundation of knowledge.

While no one can talk about the Great Reformation without talking about the Renaissance, no one can date the Renaissance precisely either. Like the Reformation, it more slid into or glided over or subtly infiltrated European ways of being than it commenced at any one given point. The changing sensibilities we recognize as the essence of "re-birth" were discernible in Italy by the beginning of the fourteenth century. The Byzantine Empire had begun its slow decline by 1204, and the products of its genius had begun their trek westward at the same time, in other words. But when a general date of its beginning in continental Europe is attached to the Renaissance, as with Luther and the Great Reformation, so here; and the actual fall of Constantinople is a strong candidate for being that point.

Tension and Conflict

It must be noted here as well that tensions between the stories and imaginations of near-Eastern culture and those of continental European culture have informed and shaped each of the West's hinge times. Characteristically and predictably, since Islam's founding in the sixth century, those tensions have been defined religiously. That is, they are most frequently spoken of as ones between Islam and Christianity, rather than being defined geographically as territorial fights. By either way of naming, the concurrence of the Great Emergence with a renewed, bellicose engagement with Islam is par for the course; and then, as now, the hands on both sides were and are equally bloody.

The whole history of the Iberian Peninsula in the fifty or sixty years before Luther is one long catalog of scrimmages between the regional Iberian kings and the Mussulmen (not to forget an equal push to drive out those other Near-Easterners, the Sephardic or Spanish Jews) leading to their expulsion, conversion, and/or slaughter. Yet the course of Christian Europe's rebirth was aided not only by the influx of Greeks fleeing Constantinople but also by the Spanish monarchs' retaking of the Moorish culture in Spain, especially of the city of Cordoba. There, in their flight, the Moors left behind a library of over four hundred thousand volumes, a wealth of knowledge far in excess of anything Christian scholars ever had access to since the destruction of the library in Alexandria. But the struggle between the two stories and two imaginations was not destined to be so easily put to rest.

The Ottomans would conquer more or less all of the southern rim of the Mediterranean even while Luther was pondering his Theses. Five years later, in 1522, they would drive the Knights of St. John, or the Hospitallers as they were popularly known, from a heavily fortified Rhodes to Malta, where we tend to think of them (when we think of them at all) as having always been, complete with a Maltese cross and an antique history. The importance of their defeat to the Europe of 1522, however, was less conversational and charming; the Hospitallers were the order of knights stationed in Rhodes specifically to defend Christian Europe from Muslim encroachment. Their defeat was the defeat of territorial, cultural, economic, and subjective safety.

Four years later, the fall of Rhodes would pale before the final fall of Hungary when the brother-in-law of the Emperor of the Holy Roman Empire would himself be killed, as would many of his bishops and clerics, not to mention thousands of his soldiers and citizenry. What was then known as Buda was destroyed, and the seeds for the contemporary conflict in Bosnia and Herzegovina were planted. Five years later, in 1529, Muslim Turks penetrated as far into Europe as Vienna, where they were eventually repulsed. They would return several times, however; and it was not until 1683 that the Ottomans were finally driven off. In that year, they managed to penetrate the city's defenses and torch about a fourth of it before they were defeated and Vienna was at last secured from further attacks.[2]

The intercultural, interreligious clashes of the late fourteenth and fifteenth centuries, combined with the rediscovery of Classical writers and the vulnerabilities of exaggerated human suffering, led the people of the peri-Reformation to a reconsideration not only of the Church but also of the state and of social and economic order. What had been merchant republics like Venice or Florence in Italy, or city-states or, in more central and northern Europe, fiefdoms and duchies, began to centralize. Especially was there a push to unify the independent duchies into something like nation-states. The impetus behind that push may have been as much the greed of hereditary political and mercantile princes as anything else, but it also had the distinct advantage of increased physical protection for increasingly productive, urban areas. The importation, and then rapidly expanding use, of gunpowder had rendered the old ways of feudal warfare pathetically obsolete. There was protection in numbers and alliances and in access to contemporary weapons wielded by contemporary soldiers, not in sword-carrying knights.

The Rise of Protestantism

The shift from manor or fiefdom or duchy organization was, for the proletariat, a shift in loyalty, identity, and social arrangement. Serfdom, which had depended on the manor and fiefdom system, disappeared; and with it, the serfs, who became the new city dwellers. No longer the property, literally or psychologically, of the lord of the manor, they now became subjects of a distant king. As subjects, they transferred their loyalty in time, but it was loyalty at a far greater remove. The ready-to-hand stability and authority of a nearby owner-lord overseeing the particulars of life was gone. As a result, each man eventually had to become more or less responsible for himself and for his own. The serf-turned-townsman came to be conceptualized as a tiny king of a tiny kingdom, a miniature of the emerging, larger political paradigm. Where once upon a time the peasant or serf or slave and all around him had been merely dependent, producing parts of a largely self-sustaining mini-economy, now the source of order and authority had to be relocated to some point within daily process. Individualism was born. Cash money, not blood and land, became the basis of power. An entrepreneurial "middle" class emerged to fill up the space between the largely bankrupt hereditary aristocracy and the abject, unempowered poverty of the peasantry. The nuclear family replaced the tribe or clan as the center of physical organization. And on and on it went.

The processes which began and solidified in the decades surrounding the Great Reformation became our new common illusion, our new shared imagination as Westerners about how the world works and how the elements of human life are to be ordered. Protestantism, when it finally arrived, was both the religious expression and the religious reflection of those processes. It survived and grew to dominance because, as the meaning-bearing part of society, it gave the reconfigurations of the late peri-Reformation their authority by sacramentalizing them during the Reformation. There is, in other words, a very good reason why most general lectures about the Great Reformation today commence with the simplistic, but accurate observation that as a hinge time, it was characterized by the rise of capitalism, of the middle class, of the nation-state, and finally of Protestantism.

It is the business of any rummage sale first to remove all of the old treasures that belonged to one's parents so as to get on with the business of keeping house the new way. As a result, there is also a very good reason why much commentary about the Great Emergence today remarks first that it has been both characterized and informed by increasing restraints upon, or outright rejections of, pure capitalism; by traditional or mainline Protestantism's loss of demographic base; by the erosion or popular rejection of the middle class's values and the nuclear family as the requisite foundational unit of social organization; by the shift from cash to information as the base of economic power; and by the demise of the nation-state and the rise of globalization. Well, of course it has been! We are holding a rummage sale, for goodness' sake! Cleaning out the whole place is the first step toward refurbishing it.

But religion in a time of reconfiguration responds to, and is informed by, more than external shifts in the consensual illusion and our human imaginings about how the world is. Indeed, more than any other construct in human life, religion is sensitive to any and every pocking that takes place in the community's story. When we look at the changes in sixteenth-century Europe's community story, we must look first at fifteenth-century Christendom's prevailing stories and specifically at how they came to be so swiftly, broadly, and violently overthrown.

The Influence of Gutenberg

The Great Reformation was intimately tied to matters of the written word from its very onset and long before Martin Luther came upon the scene. John Wycliffe, who died in 1384, was one of the peri-Reformation's more radical clerics. An Englishman, Wycliffe probably did not create the Bible that bears his name; but he undoubtedly inspired its creation by his followers. Certainly, for as long as he lived, he argued the case for presenting Scripture in the common tongue. But Wycliffe's cause, powerfully presented as it was, was limited in a way that the messages of the later reformers would not be. Wycliffe lived before Gutenberg. They lived after him.

It would, quite literally, be impossible to exaggerate the central importance to the Great Emergence of the Internet and the World Wide Web. By the same token and in absolutely analogous ways, it would be impossible to overstate the importance to the Great Reformation of the invention of the printing press by Gutenberg in 1440 and his subsequent development of movable type and oil-based inks. We laud today, almost to the point of tedium, Gutenberg and the fact that his inventiveness made Holy Writ more or less available to everyone, thereby enabling *sola scriptura* and the priesthood of all believers.

We recognize, correctly, the enormous significance of the Gutenberg or Mazarin Bible as both the beginning of the Age of the Printed Book and also the commencement of the relocation, to the book, of authority in human affairs. What we often forget to mention is that Gutenberg's converted winepress with its trays of movable type and more permanent ink was what made it possible, seventy-five years later, for Luther's Theses to jump down from the door of Wittenberg's church and circulate to people hundreds of miles away. The same Gutenberg process also allowed those distant readers to write, print, and circulate, in multiple copies to multiple readers, their own thoughts, reactions, and additions to what Luther was saying.

For that matter, we tend to forget, too, that much of the passion as well as the theological underpinnings of the Reformation was disseminated by means of popular music. With the Great Reformation, as has been true with the Great Emergence, music was often a more effectual vehicle of transmittal than was the learned treatise or the well-honed sermon. It was so effectual, in fact, that one of the first things the Roman Catholic Church did to counterattack the surge of Protestantism in the decades immediately after Luther was to address the issue of musicology. Gone, by decree, were the unintelligible elaborations that had been the pride of the Latin liturgy. In were the semantically open, more restrained works that taught as well as impressed.[3]

Because we so honor the printing press as the means by which the Bible became available to every believer, we sometimes forget something else as well. We forget, almost by default, that, decades before Luther, far more than the Bible was circulating, like a brush fire out of control, among Europe's readers. In the closing years of the fourteenth century, men like Niccolò Machiavelli (1469–1527) were thinking deeply, and writing influentially, about theories of sound governance and moral leadership that were more pragmatic than holy. The push toward realism and away from Platonic idealism was rampant. Christian/Aristotelean emphasis on teleology or some vague but vital final cause for the whole panorama of human existence was being jettisoned for a mechanical philosophy of empiricism. Combined with the West's increased access to mathematics, that attitudinal shift in fairly rapid order made way for Copernicus, whose attack upon the story was, for many, to be the most unholy of all.

In 1514, three years before Wittenberg, Copernicus, a clergyman as well as an astronomer, gave written (though not at that time published) form to the heretical idea that the sun, not the earth, was the center of the universe and that, because of that, the earth was no more than just another planet circling the larger sun. Copernicus's theory, which he developed and gave fuller expression to in 1543, was just a theory at first. Like Darwin's early musings about evolution, Copernican astronomy would be confirmed by later scientists, in Copernicus's case by men like Kepler and Galileo and Newton. Yet even as theory it was compelling enough to shatter not only the common illusion about how the world worked but also, and more disastrously, the accepted story about how it was constructed and why.

We forget sometimes that such blows level everybody, reformer and reformed alike. One of the great curmudgeons of Lutheranism, Andreas Osiander, somehow managed to attach, without Copernicus's knowledge, a foreword to *Concerning the Revolutions of the Heavenly Bodies* (once it was finally printed) that asserted the whole thing was no more than hypothetical, having no relation to reality. Yet the significant point here just may be that, because of the printing press and the access to the work of others which it enabled, every learned man who wished to, could read Copernicus and, just as readily, Osiander's foreword of rebuttal. Public cacophony was the result. Shades of Darwinism and the Great Emergence.

Rethinking Church Authority

Copernicus's theory was hardly the only body blow to the story that had prevailed between the Great Schism and the Great Reformation. For one thing, that fool Columbus had insisted on sailing west, the tragedy for the story being that he failed to fall off the edge of the earth. There is, of course, a good deal of doubt about just how many thinking men really believed the earth was flat by the time Columbus decided to test the assumption. The operative point is, instead, that common folk probably thought so and that, without doubt, the Church's cosmology and theology had been solidly grounded on a flat earth, a tiered universe, and the centrality of Earth to the creation. What the parish priest had taught for centuries put Heaven above and in several rings of ascending grandeur, and then put Hell below, likewise in several descending levels of horror. A round earth might encircle Hell in some way, but where was Heaven? Where was God, if He were no longer right upstairs? Was there, to use Amerigo Vespucci's words, really a "New

World" out there that neither the Church nor humankind had ever known of before? Had Christian priests and the holy fathers been subject to error and ignorance all along? Was the Church capable of being wrong?

Yes.

It was that simple and that devastating.

The story was broken, the common imagination dispelled into a thousand wisps of half-remembered and now ludicrous fantasy.

But in such a time, always there emerge the ideas and the clerics who will repair the rips in first the mesh sleeve and then the waterproof casing. There will be an adjusted, largely new, story and an adjusted, largely new, imagination. For the Great Reformation, once it had fully arrived, *sola scriptura* and the priesthood of all believers were two of those repairs, but they were only two among many. Luther was one such cleric, but he too was but one among many.

The number and order of the sacraments, the role of faith and works in salvation, the buying of Church positions and of forgiveness, the nature of the host and what it was by inherent constitution, the proper instruments of prayer, the efficacious timing of baptism, even the correct numbering and definition of the Ten Commandments . . . the list goes on and on, all of its items having to do with the reframing and reconceptualizing of the story and the imaginative consensus. What we so blithely name as "Reformation Protestantism" was theologically a many-headed hydra. By the same token, it was also many-armed.

Before the dust of reformation had all died down, the unity of Luther's vision of a reshaped Church was already transmuted into a Protestantism that was itself broken into Lutheran, Reformed/Calvinist/Presbyterian, Anglican, and Anabaptist Protestantism. Each of them would splinter as well, feathering out into innumerable divisions and often warring, daughter sects. Likewise, there were many men and even a woman or two who rose to positions of leadership that at the time rivaled that of Luther. Some came to support and expand Luther's work; others rose up to bitterly oppose it—Philipp Melanchthon, Ulrich Zwingli, John Calvin, Martin Bucer, Matthias and Katharina Schütz Zell, Heinrich Bullinger, Richard Hooker, the roll call of their names is almost without end. Shared sensibilities and common theological affinities did not prevent their dissenting, one from another, either. Luther, in particular, was a contentious antagonist, at one point calling John Calvin a "cow," Bullinger a "bull," and proclaiming that Zwingli was from the Evil One simply because the two of them differed violently on the true nature of the host or bread of the eucharist.

Such compliments were frequently returned then, just as they tend to be volleyed back and forth in our own time. The work of God may be pure, but its earthly application, as often as not, isn't. That certainly was made clear not only in the Great Reformation, but also in the Counter-Reformation that was Rome's response to it.

Counter-Reformation

The Counter-Reformation is also called the Catholic Reformation, the choice depending largely on whether one is Protestant or Roman Catholic. By either name, the phenomenon being referred to is one of reaction. The truth of the thing is that the late fifteenth and early sixteenth century thrust toward reform in the Church was not "Protestant" per se in the beginning. It simply was a push toward change that, in the end, managed to burst out in two directions. Luther and his fellows, believing deeply in the Church and in its urgent need of reform, pushed forward and out from the extant Church with a vision of what it could become. At the same time, however, other men like John Colet and Gasparo Contarini or the churchmen who composed the Fifth Lateran Council pushed inward to clean up and out what was already there. Protestantism resulted from the first. A renewed—or to use Butler Bass's term, a re-traditioned—Roman Catholicism flowed out of the second.

Like many other things we have noted, the tension toward changing things externally into new forms, as opposed to reworking them internally into what should be, has been a major characteristic of each of our previous hinge times and will continue to be part of our present one. The imperative for us in the twenty-first century, therefore, is not to fear either of the two coursings, but to fear with all our hearts and minds and souls the pattern of bloodiness that has in the past characterized the separation of innovators and re-traditioners from one another.

The Catholic Reformation can hardly be said to have been anything other than beneficial in many ways not only for Roman Catholics but also for the Protestors as well. It was the passion of counter-reform that gave all of Christendom the beauty of the Spanish mystics. St. John of the Cross and Teresa of Ávila belong here and come directly out of this tension, for instance, as does much of French spirituality. The Jesuits, without whom so much of Western history would be diminished, were founded by St. Ignatius Loyola in direct response to the needs of the Church and were authorized by Pope Paul III in 1540 for the same reason. The five Councils of Trent were godly assemblies of churchmen trying to purify both doctrine and practice. Matters from private devotion to corporate celebration of the mass to indulgences and to even Purgatory itself, along with dozens of other things in between, were addressed, clarified, and largely purified by the Council. And out of the Fifth (and last) Council in 1562–63 came some of the same major reforms that Luther would have loudly applauded, had he lived to see them. Seminaries were established for the actual training of clergy, something the Protestors had seen as absolutely essential. A system of appointment for bishops and dioceses that was based on vocation and not birthright was instituted. The various factions within the episcopacy—Imperial, Papal, Spanish, and French bishops—were drawn into something approximating a unity of purpose. The reform was genuine, sincere, and in many ways beneficent.

Seeking Hegemony

We can not look, however, at the huge gifts to Western civilization of either Protestantism or a renewed Roman Catholicism without looking as well at how our forebears on both sides of the divide chose competition over cooperation. Hegemony, by definition, can belong only to one among, and above, others. Pride of place, it is called; and it drove all the contenders who were the Great Reformation, just as it had always driven the contenders in Christianity's previous eras of upheaval. Five hundred years before the Great Reformation, we called the wars that followed the Great Schism by the name of "Crusades." By choosing that name, our Christian forebears colored their wars as a holy campaign to rescue Jerusalem and the Middle East from Islam. They neglected to mention, of course, to themselves or to us, that by "rescue" they meant "placed under the control of Christianity in general and Western Christianity in particular." When we come to the resolution and spin-down of the Great Reformation, we find the drive to war called by several names.

The revival and revitalization of the Inquisition, especially in Italy and Spain, is perhaps the most vicious of those presentations. The marriage of doctrinal purity with political loyalties is always an unholy union, even in the best of circumstances. In the case of the Reformation and Counter-Reformation, it took on a singular vicious-ness and horror. And the bloodiest of the contentions we label the Thirty Years' War. By the time it and the Dutch Revolt—also known as the Eighty Years' War—were more or less concluded in 1648 by the Treaty of Münster and later the Peace of Westphalia, almost half of Europe's citizenry would be dead. Now, a rummage sale later, we can not—must not—shake our heads, as if in confusion about how such things could ever have been and then, with an assumed innocence, look the other way. Those who do not learn from the past, it has been wisely said, are destined to relive it.

---

1. *The Reformation: A History*, which was published in the United States in 2004 by Viking, immediately comes to mind here. Magnificent in its scope and in the beauty of its sympathetic attention to detail, *The Reformation* was written by Diarmaid MacCulloch, professor of the history of the Church at Oxford and a fellow of the British Academy. It is now generally regarded as one of the great works of historical scholarship. MacCulloch dates the end of the peri-Reformation and the beginning of the Great Reformation from the late 1400s.

2. It would be another century, though, before far and away the greatest killer in Europe's history was finally worn down more than defeated. One of the oddities of our cyclical upheavals is that they have always been accompanied by some great, generalized, human illness. Labeled by historians as "pandemics," there had been only three recorded ones prior to our own time. The first occurred in the fifth and sixth centuries, the second between the eighth and fourteenth. The third was the devouring distress most commonly known to us as the Black Death.

Like our own contemporary struggle with HIV-AIDS (which is now being labeled as a fourth pandemic by some authorities) but many, many times more virulent, the Black Death was rampant across the known world during all the years of the entire Great Reformation from peri- to post-. By 1340 it had penetrated Europe and can not really be said to have subsided until 1771 when the Great Plague of Moscow appears to have been its culmination. In those four hundred-plus years, it would kill over seventy-five million people in Europe alone, the worldwide toll being unknown.

The result of such devastation and human vulnerability was—and inevitably always is—a generalized reconsideration of the efficacy of the Church and the worth of resources extended to it. Likewise, there were and always are shifts in the popular as well as clerical understanding about the purposes of religion in general and of its temporal rewards in particular. Whether the recurrence of pandemics simultaneously with the recurrence of ecclesial upheavals is pure coincidence or whether, as some would have it, there is some other connection is for a later and more adequately informed time to determine. At the moment, all that can be said is that there is a co-occurrence between history's pandemics and our times of re-formation.

3. One need only watch the creative struggles of Palestrina, the great Roman composer of the sixteenth century (ca. 1526–94), to see the power of this shift at work. As the Roman Church went through its time of re-traditioning in the Counter-Reformation, one of the principles laid down by the Council of Trent was indeed a severe ban on the polyphonic treatment of sacred texts that had previously characterized the Roman liturgy. Palestrina is often hailed today, as he was in his own time, as the savior of "Church" music, however; for it was Palestrina who managed to create such great polyphonic masterworks—see, for example, his *Missa Papae Marcelli* or "Pope Marcellus Mass"—that their aesthetic impact overrode the anathema of their not being semantically accessible. On the other hand, one has only to look at the collected works of Monteverdi (1567–1643), ordained Roman priest and widely acknowledged creator or father of modern music, to expose the broader and opposite impact of having a people's music in holy space. And it was Gutenberg's press that enabled the spread of those Protestant hymns that even the great Palestrina could not entirely counter and of the operas and madrigals by which the great Monteverdi later spoke his homilies to a re-traditioning Church.

4

Questions of Re-formation

Darwin, Freud, and the Power of Myth

We can discuss with dispassion the confusions and anguish of some-
one else's earlier hinge time, but can we discuss with anything even
close to objective dispassion the confusions and anguish of our own?
Probably not, especially if we jump right into analyzing where we are
at this point in time. But we can, with a minimum of effort, climb
up on the back of the last century or so of history and take a fairly
clear sighting of how North American Christians got from where
we were to where we are; and perspective generally alleviates anxiety
enough to make the effort of climbing worthwhile.

The simultaneous pocking of our story and our consensual illusion
as North American (and also, in this case, as Western) Christians is
the result of persistent bombardment from many sources. Yet even
given that plethora, few if any religion scholars and analysts have
trouble naming Science as the principal agent of successful challenge
to a story and an imagination that had been in place, more or less

securely, from the post-Reformation right up until the middle of the nineteenth century.

Darwin ... and Faraday

When exactly, in the mid-1800s, the die was cast, depends on whom one asks. Most commonly, lay analysts point to 1859 and the publication of Darwin's *The Origin of Species* as the tipping point that sent us careening off into new cultural, social, political, and theological territory. Physicists themselves, however, tend to place the pivot point at 1851. In that year, Michael Faraday stepped down as professor of chemistry at the Royal Military Academy in Woolwich, England. In the sixteen years between Faraday's retirement from active teaching and his death in 1867, his theories and discoveries about field theory came to capture the popular imagination in a way that they had previously not done.

Most North Americans know who Darwin was. Most of us even have opinions about his theory of evolution (though relatively few of us have read what he had to say in his own words when he said it). Almost none of us, however, talk about, let alone read, Michael Faraday. Yet Faraday did as much to rattle the bars of premodernity as did anyone short of Darwin and Einstein themselves.

What he did in the years of his active life as a teaching chemist, among other things, was to discover and describe electromagnetic rotations and electromagnetic induction, the principle on which electric transformers and electric generators work. In effect, what that meant was that electricity ceased to be an interesting toy and became the base for almost every part of the technology that first spawned and then enabled the postmodernism within which the Great Emergence is coalescing. At a more immediately theological level, Faraday contended that there was no ether and no matter, as physical substances. There were, instead, fields of forces like electricity and magnetism and gravity that, albeit unseen, girded everything. When and where the invisible lines of the force fields intersected, they created matter, light being no more than the vibration or motion of the intersecting forces. So much for mystery and angels or spirits descending in light or as light. So much for leaving the invisible as too divine to tamper with. So much for thinking that everything that looked miraculous really was.

Whether one says that it was Faraday's work or Darwin's theory that marks the beginning of the shifts leading to the Great Emergence is of little moment, actually. The two of them together are, without question, the line of demarcation between post-Reformation and peri-Emergence ways of thinking, being, and believing. They also embodied what would become two of the major member-disciplines or components of twentieth-century science: biology and physics (though Faraday would probably have been confused to find the latter label applied to his work). In consort with each other and the sciences that came out of them, biology and physics were to split the cable open, tear the story, snag the sleeve, and lay out to public view the braided strand.

The word *biologist* does not itself appear in English until 1874. By that time, however, Darwinian theory had already begun to seep into theological as well as academic conversation. Within twenty years, the threat of evolution and the kind of biblical criticism and liberal theology it and other concomitant trends were seen as empowering had reached such a pitch that a series of Bible Conferences of Conservative Protestants were held at various sites in the United States. In 1895, the Conference of Conservative Protestants, meeting in Niagara Falls, issued a statement of five principles necessary to claim true Christian belief: the inerrancy of the Scripture; the divinity of Jesus Christ; the historicity of the Virgin birth; the substitutionary nature of the Atonement; and the physical, corporeal return of Jesus, the Christ. Those five principles of doctrine would become "the Fundamentals." By 1910, the Conservative Protestants body would begin publishing a magazine called *The Fundamentals*; and the word *fundamentalist* would enter our language as the label for a very clearly defined mind-set. Such clarity has feathered out a bit in the century since, but the five principles of the Niagara meeting, along with the two others of the obligation to evangelize and belief in Jesus as a personal savior, have held firm as the core of evangelical Christianity.

One of the Great Emergence's central thrusts over the closing decades of the twentieth century and since has been to attempt an accommodation between the fundamentals of the evangelicalism out of which many Emergents have come and the theology of the more religiously and culturally diverse Great Emergence itself. Among the first, major accommodations that has to transpire early in a hinge time is this very process. That which has held hegemony, finding itself under attack, always must drop back, re-entrench itself, run up its colors in defiance, and demand that the invaders attack its stronghold on its own terms. In religion as in warfare, things never quite work out that way; but there is a period in which the invaders do hesitate, trying to figure out how and why, with guns in their hands, they should want to attack the fort with bows and arrows, or something very analogous to that.

Freud, Jung, and Campbell

But biology and/or medicine were creating more mayhem than just a backward-looking evolutionary thought or explanation. Born in 1856, Sigmund Freud, before he was done, would open up to public view a whole new landscape, namely that of the unconscious. While the concept of conscious versus unconscious states of being was as old as religion itself—it can be found in Vedic literature, for example—Freud's genius was in building constructs or models of "mind" that, by their very articulation, demanded further investigation. In a sense, Freud was the Amerigo Vespucci of the Great Emergence: he declared beyond refute the presence of a whole New World which, it is fair to say, was effectively unknown to, and unperceived by, earlier eras of human history.

After Freud, Carl Jung, born in Switzerland in 1875, extended the exploration of this New World and achieved what Freud did not. That is, Jung's was a steadier, less neurotic and prickly personality, and his writings were accessible to laity and scholars alike. He built on Freud, certainly, but his paintings and word-sketches of the subjective life were mystical enough and lyrical enough to entice readers who would never have paid more than passing attention to Freud. And Jung opened the forest beyond Freud's beachhead by speaking of a collective unconscious, just as he further opened up the concept of libido that was primal soil for both.

Jung's career would be generative, as well, not only in terms of his own writing, but also in terms of his enormous influence on later thinkers. He was a motivating force behind Joseph Campbell, for example. It would be very difficult, in speaking of the coming of the Great Emergence, to overestimate the power of Campbell in the disestablishment of what is called "the Christian doctrine of particularity" and "Christian exclusivity." That doctrine and principle, in duet, hold that Jesus and Jesus only is God-among-us and that there is no salvation for humankind anywhere anytime independent of belief in Jesus. Both those dogmas held almost total, popular sway in the early and mid-1900s in North American Christianity. It was Campbell who would first successfully challenge and, near the end of the twentieth century, successfully begin to rout them in popular thought. But then, Campbell, like Luther, had an advantage that

Freud, like Wycliffe, did not. Campbell had a new technology of mass communication infinitely better than any that Freud had ever even dreamed of having.

The Advent of Radio and Television

The telegraph, when it came into general use—thanks, of course, to Michael Faraday and others, like James Clerk Maxwell, who followed him—was a huge boon to the rapid exchange of information in a way that was more or less analogous to the first exchanges empowered by Gutenberg's earliest presses. Radio, when it came into broad, popular use in the 1930s, was another major leap forward. Far more ubiquitous than the telegraph and far easier to produce and transmit copy for, it became Everyman's (and Everywoman's) contact with a larger world that had previously been "known about" only somewhat after the fact and "experienced" not at all. Now the world was just a dial away. But by the mid-1940s, there was television . . . expensive, snowy screened, demanding of time, but there. Really there. A movie theater in one's living room, a world at one's fingertips, just waiting to be both seen and heard.

Bishop Fulton J. Sheen was probably the first professional religionist to realize the immense potential of television as a means for shaping religion in the laity; but in impact, the bishop was an amateur compared to Joseph Campbell. Campbell, born in 1904 and a scholar in the fields of comparative mythology and comparative religion, taught for thirty-eight years at Sarah Lawrence College. During those years, he produced a number of books, but two of them in particular were to change the course of American Christianity. The four-volume set, *The Masks of God*, and his magnum opus, *The Hero with a Thousand Faces*, were and are authoritative attacks (whether that was the motivation behind their composition, or not) upon

Christian exclusivity and particularity. How deep and broad and lasting the influence of those books would have been, had they been left to stand alone, no one will ever now know.

In his late seventies and early eighties, well after his retirement from Sarah Lawrence, Campbell teamed up with Bill Moyers to produce a PBS series entitled *The Power of Myth*. Campbell died after the filming was complete but before the series was aired, so he never lived to see the confirmation of his belief that it was in television that one educated and shaped a culture's thought. And shape it did. The universality and commonality of religious thought and sensibilities was spread out across America's living rooms for all to see. University-educated professional and high school dropout alike were being taught by two of the nation's most skilled communicators; and in due time, the inevitable result was a direct assault from the pew onto the pulpit.

The popularity of *The Power of Myth* rested certainly on its excellence and in part on Moyers's genius as well as Campbell's. The series, at the time of this writing, still stands as the single, most popular and most frequently purchased one in PBS's history. But it also triggered a whole new generation of expanded readership for Campbell's books; and together, books and series persuaded much of North American Christendom that exclusivity and particularity were a hard, if not an impossible, sell. What of *solus christus,* not to mention *sola scriptura*?

A challenge that would have been rejected by believers as clerical heresy had it been delivered from the pulpit was now being listened to and thought about and talked about around watercoolers and over backyard fences. Why? In large part because Campbell and Moyers had understood that hearing something when one is in one's own home, relaxed among one's own family and surroundings, enjoying not only a bit of rest in one's easy chair but also perchance a bit of refreshment as well, is vastly and effectually different from hearing the same thing in public and sacrosanct space while sitting, dressed for show, among one's social associates or—God forbid—one's betters. The mind comes out to play with the imagination in the former; it dare not come out at all in the latter, at least not visibly.

But as powerful as Campbell's influence on popular as well as scholarly religious thought has been over the decades since his death, another part of Jung's legacy has been equally powerful in a more indirect way. In fairness, we should speak in this regard not of Jung's work alone but of Jung in concert, not only with Freud's legacy, but also with the early or transitional work of men and women like Alfred Adler, Otto Rank, Karen Horney, Erik Erikson, and others who built on the work of either or both of them.

The New Self

As these thinkers and experimenters, and many, many other gifted scholars like them, pushed farther and farther into the interior, their efforts attracted the interest of whole coteries of other scientists—of biologists, psychologists, neuroscientists, physicians, linguists, anthropologists, artists, physicists, and philosophers—all of whom in one way or another began to question the old, standing definitions of "self." Equally important is the fact that the experts in these fields of relatively established sciences were joined by men and women who were expert in fields of science that had not even existed two or three human generations earlier . . . experts in electronic computation, in computer science, the Internet/the World Wide Web/www 2.0, in chaos math and network theory, in nanotechnology, in artificial intelligence, in post-human theory and ethics.

It was a revolution in progress right in front of our very eyes and in full view of anyone who wanted to flip something, whether that something be the pages of a popular book, magazine or newspaper, or simply the switches on a television set, a radio, a computer, or a cell phone. This revolution was not happening in some faraway land or behind some curtain of distance and esoteric learnedness, either. This one was in your face, up close, and personal, because this one taunts every one of us . . . who are you, there in the mirror? . . . what are you, human or machine, agent and actor or puppet and victim? . . . . how do you know? . . . what does it mean, this "knowing" thing? . . . how do you know you know? . . . yoo-hoo, who's in there and where?

We had long known (at least, in the centuries since medicine began doing autopsies, anyway) that René Descartes' theory of a homunculus "self" resident somewhere in the center-brain in each of us was foolishness. In the 1640s, Descartes had satisfied the angst of post-Reformation imagination quite effectively by postulating that very thing, however. He had taught that body and mind are two entirely different things, *res extensa* and *res cogitans*. Like some twenty-first-century night watchman monitoring his TV screens in the lobby of a skyscraper, Descartes said there was a "self," a little person separate from every part of the body, that monitored events and governed individual human existence and conduct. Descartes proved his own existence as a "self" to himself by his now-clichéd axiom of "*Cogito, ergo sum*—I think, therefore I am." That woefully inadequate definition of our humanness is now spoken of by cognitive scientists as "The Cartesian Error" or "Descartes' Error," or even, sometimes, as "René's Folly."[1]

The term *cognitive science* was not even around until 1973, when it was first used in conjunction with work in artificial intelligence. As a label, however, it was destined to spread rapidly and encompass much. The result is that the cognitive sciences now include a vast array of subdisciplines and burgeoning areas of research, all of them having to do with Descartes's old anathema: What are we/what am I? Is there even such a thing as the "self"? Is "mind" the same as, or different from, "brain"? If so, how can "I" be? More to the point, how can "I" be held responsible for anything anywhere anytime? If not, then what is "mind" and where does it dwell and of what is it made? The questions are endless, as are the media sources willing and able to broadcast them, unanswered, into every North American life.

Who, indeed, asks the citizen of these times, goes to my prayers when I pray? Where in me is the responsible part? Where is that same part in the front-page murderer or in my neighbor, the pedophile? What does God exist in relation to? What is a soul and what do we mean when we say we work to save something that may not even be? Et cetera, et cetera, et cetera, until we are as sick of the questions as we are of the anguish and confusion from which they come.

Essential Questions

But even our sense of existential sickness and near defeat are as they should be.

That is to say, they are of one piece with the historic pattern that we are once more reenacting. Each time of re-formation has the same central question: Where, now, is the authority? But each reconfiguration also has at least two dominant, unrelenting questions that attend it and may or may not be unique to it. The question of "Where now is our authority?" is the fundamental or foundational question of all human existence and/or endeavor, be it individual or that of a larger, social unit. Without an answer to it, the individual personality or the personality of the group at large alike fall into disarray and ultimate chaos. It is Hell where there is no answer to that question.

The two or more questions that are particular to any one, given re-formation era are of a somewhat lesser magnitude, not in the agitation they evoke, but in the focus of their answers. They are, in a sense, always subsets of the authority question. Once answered, they become vehicles of a sort for transmitting the identity of the newly established authority into the politics, economics, learned disciplines, cohesive culture, and legal norms of a society as well as into its religious institutions and codes. Religion empowers the answers by sanctifying them; but it is itself not so much defined by those answers as it is characterized by them. It is the authority answer which defines.

The two overarching, but complementary questions of the Great Emergence are: (1) What is human consciousness and/or the humanness of the human? and (2) What is the relation of all religions to one another—or, put another way, how can we live responsibly as devout and faithful adherents of one religion in a world of many religions? Those torturous questions, which have bobbed along in human history for centuries, now come to us with a militant ferocity, a ferocity that enjoys a line of direct, uninterrupted descent straight down from Michael Faraday and Charles Darwin. The other great truth here is that we can not be said to have truly entered into any kind of post-Emergence stability until we have answered both of them.

The assertive presence in general conversation of the central question of authority is evidence that a re-formation is in process. The assertive presence in general conversation nowadays of two, equally unresolved but clearly defined and related, secondary questions is evidence that this particular re-formation of ours is deep into process. We have looked at the two or three intellectual and technological tsunamis of the last hundred and fifty years that determined the nature and definition of what our secondary questions would be. Obviously, those disruptions in the cultural and intellectual status quo have contributed energy and urgency also to the larger question of where authority should be located. But before we begin to look at the Great Emergence itself and how it may be expected to address our re-formation questions, we need to look at one other part of the puzzle.

Emerging Christians are the immediate products of the twentieth century. What they see, what they do, and the materials with which they work were all shaped by a particular place in time and space. What they can imagine and even what they can actually accomplish will likewise be both characterized and enabled by the context of a particular culture present in a particular time. Before we look at the Great Emergence itself, then, we need to consider, at least briefly, a few of the major cultural shifts in the twentieth century that have determined the religious and ecclesial perspectives out of which emergents are working.

An overview like the one that follows here is hardly the sum of our current situation, nor is it the whole of what is and is making the Great Emergence. Quite the contrary. The full list of precipitating and defining events runs somewhere in excess of three dozen discrete and distinct items. Some of those shifts—the ones we will look at—are so major that they can not be glossed over by a simple listing. Some of them can be. Others of them may best be served by waiting for a longer, more detailed treatment than this one. For the purposes of a general overview, however, it hopefully will suffice if we look chronologically at a select few of the more obvious pivotal events or changes that violated the cable of post-Reformation meaning and exposed its braided strands to the rough handling of the last decades of the twentieth century and the opening one of the twenty-first.[2]

---

1. It should be noted here, just as an aside, that theologians do not use quite so disparaging a tone in dealing with the consequences of Descartes' theories of God. Descartes thought that God had to exist and that His existence could

be proved simply because he—or any one of us—contained the idea of God and of perfections of beingness that are qualities of God and could only come into us from Him. Labeled as such or not, this argument likewise seems now to be somewhere between ludicrous and dauntingly cerebral.

2. *The Great Emergence*, its questions, and its causes are being treated here, of course, as a Christian phenomenon, and primarily in terms of North American Christianity. That focusing of the lens should not be interpreted as meaning that North American Judaism has not undergone the same shifts and emerged with many of the same questions and analogous results, because it has. Likewise, Western Christianity in general, as we have already noted, has shared many of the same burdens and joys as has North American Christianity, though the two are culturally distinct enough to justify not including both here.

5

The Century of Emergence

Einstein, the Automobile, and the Marginalization of Grandma

Albert Einstein dominates every part of the twentieth century including, and more or less directly, religion. He began his significant work in 1902, but it is 1905 that is known as *Annus Mirabilis*, the year always to be marveled at. In that year Einstein published four papers that changed the consensual illusion forever.

First, he postulated that the photoelectric effect could be explained if light were understood as being at times "bundles," or what he called "quanta," interacting with matter. Max Planck, another mighty giant of the century, had introduced such an idea in 1900 on the basis of hypothetical mathematics, but it was Einstein who gave us the quantum world incarnated. And as surely as Newton had once upon a time postulated the classical physics that was the descriptor of the visible world, so Einstein's students, associates, and even some detractors would give us the quantum physics that was the descriptor of the invisible world. As had been true with Faraday's work, so again much of the kingdom of the angels, of the mystery of soul, was forever breached by the simple process of being exposed as physical and subject to incredible, but still describable, laws.

In the *Annus Mirabilis*, Einstein also published a paper on Brownian motion, though he apparently was unaware at first that the phenomenon he was studying went by that name. Robert Brown, who died in 1859, had been a friend and confidant of Darwin. He was also a crotchety, but methodical, botanist who first noticed that any small, small bit of anything—dead or alive—will zig and zag about frantically when it is suspended in a liquid. Because he described that fact, the zigging and zagging is named after him—Brownian motion.

Amateur as well as professional scientists had already played with, and commented upon, Brownian motion for half a century before Einstein ever decided to try to describe quantitatively the nature of the motion. In his study, though, Einstein demonstrated that the movement of tiny things in liquid suspension is proof of molecular activity and, as a result, offered almost irrefutable support for the existence of atoms. The angst of the mid-twentieth century had been born. Welcome to the birthing cries of a world that understood, for the first time in human history, that we really could destroy the earth and each other totally, completely, without hope of escape. Welcome to Hiroshima.

In the third of his 1905 papers, Einstein—brilliant, sassy, and twenty-six years old—published the theory that, over the course of his lifetime, would cause him the greatest consternation. Based on his work on the electrodynamics of moving things, Einstein postulated the "special theory of relativity." In effect, what special relativity did was overthrow any notion that there might be such a thing as absolute space or absolute time by showing that both are dependent upon an observer and that each of them is perceived differently, depending on the observer doing the observing.

Heisenberg and Uncertainty

The special theory led Einstein to argue, in his fourth paper, that matter and energy, which had always been thought to be separate entities, were equivalent, giving the world what is perhaps its most famous scientific formula: $E = mc^2$. But the special theory also led, in 1927, to what undeniably is the most famous principle in twentieth-century science—Heisenberg's Uncertainty Principle. It was this that would break the heart of Einstein and, in many ways, that of his century.

The Heisenberg Uncertainty Principle has been reduced, by now, to an almost commonplace tidbit of everyday conversation: You can measure the speed of something (in Heisenberg's case, a particle) or you can measure its position; but you can not measure them both. That is, the more you know about the speed of a thing, the less you know about its position until finally one has to concede that the act of observing itself changes the thing observed.

Einstein saw Heisenberg's Uncertainty as a corruption, and even a reprehensible misuse, of his special theory of relativity, arguing that it destroyed the basis for any "fact" in life. Einstein was right in his interpretation of the consequences, but Heisenberg was right in his science. Nor would the Heisenberg Principle stay safely tucked away in physics labs. Instead, "uncertainty" became the only fact that could be accepted as fact, not only in the popular mind, but also in large segments of the academic mind as well.

In particular, literary deconstruction planted its standard dead in the center of Heisenberg, claiming that there is no absolute truth, only truth relative to the perceiver. And, as an obvious consequence, all writing—be it sacred or secular—has no innate meaning until it is read and, therefore, has no meaning outside of the circumstances and disposition of the reader. Enter the battle of The Book. Enter the warriors, both human and inanimate, who will hack the already wounded body of *sola scriptura* into buriable pieces. Enter the twentieth century's great, garish opening in the cable's waterproof casing of story.[1]

Looking for the Real Jesus

But in the name of historical accuracy as well as fairness, we need to remind ourselves, before we go any further, that "Scripture only and only Scripture" really was, if not badly wounded, then certainly badly bruised, well before Einstein or Heisenberg ever came along. Their work would only reinforce and broaden an investigation already in progress.

At about the time this country was being established, a German theologian, Hermann Samuel Reimarus, first asked the question that would haunt the twentieth century far more than it ever haunted his own. Basically, what Reimarus asked himself and his colleagues was a deceptively simple question: What, he said, if Jesus of Nazareth and the Jesus of Western history and thought are not the same?

Although Reimarus eventually wrote a masterful treatise, *The Aims of Jesus and His Disciples*, to address the subject, neither his question nor his carefully considered responses unsettled many folk at the time, simply because they had little or no access to either Reimarus or his ideas. His basic question, however, would prove to be like the miseries in Pandora's box; once it had been articulated, there was no putting it back in the recesses of academic halls and moldering libraries ever again. Most auspiciously, it would be asked in print again in 1901 by Albert Schweitzer in a book called *The Quest for the Historical Jesus*.

Schweitzer, unlike Reimarus, was a popular public figure, an organist of some international stature, at that time, as well as a clergyman. He lived, as well, in the early twentieth century, when the beginnings of mass communication—cheap books, ubiquitous newspapers, a reliable and inexpensive postal service—made it harder to keep ideas contained, especially if they were a bit scandalous or insurrectionist. And Schweitzer's ideas were; for he concluded that Jesus of Nazareth was not the same entity as the Christ of Western Christianity and Western thought. He concluded as well that we could never know that "real" or historical Jesus. As a result of its huge, popular impact, Schweitzer's *Quest* is usually regarded now as marking the end of one era in *sola scriptura* and empowering the opening of another.

Some four decades later, before the midcentury, scholars would begin to theorize, using literary deconstruction and form criticism, just where and how editors or redactors had changed original texts into those we today recognize as the canonical Gospels. Others would work to physically discover and define the accumulating layers of text that undergird the editions we have. The discoveries of Nag Hammadi and Qumran in 1945 and 1947 respectively, along with more recent archaeological finds, would furnish primary sources in physical support of much of what earlier had been only theory. By the closing decades of the twentieth century, Jesus scholarship, with Reimarus, Schweitzer, and Heisenberg as its intellectual forebears, had become the life work, in public space, of superb *and* popularizing scholars like Marcus Borg, John Dominic Crossan, Elaine Pagels, and Karen King.

What their work in aggregate seemed to offer up to public view was a Jesus who was as much guru and sage as God Incarnate. In response, other, equally well-known and popularly published thinkers and researchers, working with the same tools and as various in background as Fr. Raymond E. Brown and Rabbi Jacob Neusner or Bishop N. T. Wright, worked to lessen the subjectivity of Jesus scholarship by focusing on the Judaism in which He lived, contending that historical context is the soundest critical tool available to us for faithful exploration and discovery. Either way, Heisenberg, had he been alive in 2000, would undoubtedly have been amazed at just how much difference a little physics can make in a village church.

And though Einstein may have deplored Heisenberg's Uncertainty Principle and correctly foreseen, unlike Heisenberg, what the cultural and religious ramifications of it would most surely be, he too can not be allowed to leave the Scripture only–only Scripture conversation scot-free. In 1915–16, Einstein published what was the last of his great papers, his "General Theory of Relativity."

Out of the mathematics of general relativity would come ideas and postulates that are themselves also matters now of household conversation: time as another, and fourth, dimension; time as capable of being slowed; the ongoing expansion of the universe; the Big Bang. And in conjunction with the work of other brilliant, popularly known physicists like Edwin Hubble, general relativity would eventually make it possible, on July 20, 1969, for Neil Armstrong and Buzz Aldrin to walk on the surface of Earth's moon. In doing so, they walked on what always before had been the footstool of God, and that made all the difference. Literalism based on inerrancy could not survive the blow (though it would die a slow and painful death); and without inerrancy-based literalism, the divine authority of Scripture was decentralized, subject to the caprices of human interpretation, turned into some kind of pick-and-choose bazaar for skillful hagglers. Where now is our authority?

Enter Pentecostalism

But if 1905 had been an *annus mirabilis*, 1906 could hardly be called a slouch either. In February of that year, a young black preacher named William Seymour left Kansas, headed toward Los Angeles and the call to come and preach his strange doctrine that baptism in the Holy Spirit was accompanied by the gift of speaking in tongues (both glossolalia and zenolalia). Within less than two weeks, the church that originally had invited Seymour to preach had barred their doors against him and his appalling doctrine, forcing him to move his sermonizing to the home of a supportive couple, Richard and Ruth Asberry. From the Asberrys' modest home on North Bonnie Brae Street in Los Angeles, Seymour preached to a small, but growing crowd without incident or fanfare until April 9. That night, during the evening sermon, one of Seymour's listeners, Edward S. Lee, suddenly spoke in tongues for the first time. Three days later, Seymour himself received the gift, as did many of the others present.

Word of what was happening on North Bonnie Brae spread like a wildfire through the Latino and Negro communities of L.A. and, shockingly enough for those days, through Caucasian ones as well. The next night, so large a crowd of every race and social class and both genders gathered on the porch of the Asberry home that the porch itself collapsed, doing damage as well to the house's foundation. Two days later, on April 14, 1906, Seymour preached his first sermon in an old, cleaned-up and converted livery stable at 312 Azusa Street, and the rest is history. The rest is soul-changing, history-changing history, in fact; Pentecostalism would become a major player in the new rummage sale.

There had been a series of pentecostal-like events before the Azusa Street Revival. Some were as far away as Wales and Switzerland, and others as close as western North Carolina. Charles Parham, whose ministry was located in Kansas, for instance, was the one who originally had taught Seymour; and Parham is still regarded today as one of the founders of Pentecostalism. It is always Azusa Street, however, that is acknowledged as its true starting point. And over the next century, Pentecostalism, Azusa Street style, would sweep not only North America but the whole globe. By 2006, the number of

Pentecostal and Charismatic Christians would exceed five hundred million, making them second only to Roman Catholicism as the world's largest Christian body.[2]

Because Pentecostalism had its roots deep in egalitarianism, it was to come into North American Christian experience as the first, visible fulfillment of the apostle's cry that "In Christ, we are all one body." Pentecostalism's demonstration of a Church of all classes and races and both genders became a kind of living proof text that first horrified, then unsettled, then convicted, and ultimately helped change congregational structure in the United States, regardless of denomination. In addition, the often loud, often apparently disorderly, always musical and participatory worship of the Pentecostal movement came in time to make the worship of the established Protestant denominations look as if they were somewhere between corseted and downright dead by boredom. Participatory worship became the standard, especially in evangelical Christianity which is Pentecostalism's nearest kin in bloodline.

The impact of the African-American experience on North American Christianity was and remains enormous. To begin even to sketch it requires a freestanding volume just on that subject alone, a largess we do not have, unfortunately. Suffice it here, then, simply to say that the Afro-American community in 1900 was, by and large, the only part of American Christianity that had an active, native, or "largely untheologized," community-accepted spirituality. One of the great gifts of Pentecostalism to the greater body of the whole Church was its origins in, and incorporation of, the African-American spiritual experience. The efficacy of historic black spirituality and the immediacy of palpable contact with the divine which it enabled have been central to Pentecostalism since Azusa Street. It is almost undoubtedly this last component of Pentecostalism that has caused it, quite literally, to encompass the globe as well as change the ways and expectations of non-Pentecostal worshipers.

All that having been said, however, we must hasten to say that in terms of the Great Emergence as an event in religio-cultural history, there is an even greater point to be made here. Pentecostalism by definition assumes the direct contact of the believer with God and, by extension, the direct agency of the Holy Spirit as instructor and counselor and commander as well as comforter. As such and stated practically, Pentecostalism assumes that ultimate authority is experiential rather than canonical. This is *not* either to say or to imply that there is denial of the Holy Scriptures. It is to say, rather, that forced into a choice between what a believer thinks with his or her own mind to be said in the Holy Scripture and an apparently contradictory message from the Holy Spirit, many a Pentecostal must prayerfully, fearfully, humbly accept the more immediate authority of the received message. The same thing is true when the contradiction occurs between a received message and the words of a pastor or bishop. Pentecostalism, in other words, offered the Great Emergence its first, solid, applied answer to the question of where now is our authority. Probably just slightly more than a quarter of emergent Christians and the emergent Church are Pentecostal by heritage or affinity, and they have brought with them into the new aggregate this central belief in the Holy Spirit as authority.

Leaving Grandma in the Rearview Mirror

Having come from so lofty a set of considerations as those about Pentecostalism, we need to look at something that appears far more mundane and less portentous, at least at first blush. That is, before we leave the early years of the twentieth century, we have to look at the automobile. It had been around for many years by the time 1900 arrived, especially in Europe where men like Karl Benz were making automotive history long before the average Americans ever even thought about driving one of the things. So it was not the automobile per se that would impact American Christianity. It was the Tin Lizzie, the Flivver, the Model T. Call it by whatever popular name you want, it came upon us in 1908, and it was affordable, reliable, easier than a horse and buggy to care for . . . and fun! America took to the roads and never looked back.

The car was a boon that, like a sharp knife, cut two ways, however. It freed Americans to roam at will, thereby loosening them from the physical ties that had bound earlier generations to one place, one piece of land, one township, one schoolhouse, and one community-owned consensual illusion, of which a large component was the community church. The affordable car enabled city dwelling in a way that had not been possible for many Americans in the past. It also provided, very early, the mechanism by which what had been the Sabbath became Sunday instead.

Family afternoons on Grandpa's front porch after Grandma's hearty Sabbath lunch gave way to spins out into the countryside with or without a Sunday picnic. Sabbath afternoons with one's kin gave way as well to carefully tabulated afternoon calls on friends who lived down the road a bit. Within a few decades, the Tin Lizzie and her offspring would so erode the Sabbath that Sunday would become the day for shopping, for mall visits, movies, and dozens of Little League games, not to mention a significant number of major league ones. Sunday evening services all but disappeared; and early Sunday morning ones (or Saturday evening ones) were invented in order to allow the faithful to get their Sabbath worship over and done with early enough so that there would still be some Sunday left to enjoy.

None of this is inherently either bad or good, so much as it just is. What we have is a set of cultural shifts that came about, in large measure, because of yet another piece of technology, in this case the automobile. What does matter, though, is that Reformation Christianity had rested for centuries on biblical literacy, the nuclear family, and the conserving effect of shared, multigenerational reading, theology, and worship. While we may, at first glance, scoff at Norman Rockwell's short, chubby, apron-clad, wispy-haired Grandmas serving feasts to multigenerational hordes, a second glance should tell us something else. When mid-twentieth-century Caucasian Protestantism lost Rockwell's Grandmas, it lost a large part of itself.

It was Grandma, in general, who asked during each Sabbath lunch exactly what little Johnny had learned in Sunday School. And while Johnny might be forgiven for occasionally fluffing a question or two, his parents most surely would not, were it to be discovered that Johnny had not even been to Sunday School in the first place. It was Grandma as well who, by and large, rode herd on the preacher and his tendency toward fancy or newfangled sermons and imported theories of God. Grandma was, in essence, a brake—a formidable one, in fact—on social/cultural/theological change. And because she was and because she asked often and directly about the biblical instruction going on in her families' homes, she served as something somewhere between the Archivist and the Enforcer of Protestant codes and sheer Bible fact and story. When the Tin Lizzie took away her kingdom of influence, it was Protestantism more than Grandma that came untethered and was diminished. We should note as well that the re-definition of traditionally female roles across all the generations was, and still is, a principal contributor to the shredding of the cable and the exposing of its parts. It certainly is one to which we shall return.

The Influence of Karl Marx

American Christianity in the first two decades of the twentieth century was directly impacted, of course, by more than scientific discoveries and technological inventions as such. Whenever the question of the rightful placement of authority begins to come into play, it is political theory that most markedly begins to change. It is, in principle anyway, the task of political theory to accommodate the secular part of the authority question by furnishing it with new answers. Unfortunately, the answers so born are never entirely secular in scope, implementation, or aftereffects.

More than one historian has remarked that the French Revolution of 1848 was born before its time. That is, it was a kind of limited (though deadly) and preliminary dry run for what was to become, less than seventy years later, the first in a series of wars that would mark the twentieth century as the bloodiest in human history. Karl Marx, with Friedrich Engels, published the *Communist Manifesto* in 1848; and Marx's fingerprints were all over the French Revolution. Despite the ferocity of that revolt and the radical propositions that lay beneath it, Marx's theories of economics and political structure did not enjoy broad circulation or really have much global impact until the closing decades of the nineteenth century.

As with Einstein, so with Marx, in that it would probably be impossible to overstate the influence he and his ideas would come to have on the world of the twentieth century. Like Einstein, Marx built upon the work of those who had come before him, being at times more a realizer than an innovator. In particular, Marx built upon the theories of George Wilhelm Friedrich Hegel. Hegel, who died when Marx was only thirteen, had taught that everything had, inherent in it, its opposite. Good and evil were not antithetical to one another, but rather were two parts of a thing that itself would exist only so long as the two were in opposition to one another. Once the two opposites in any thing had resolved their conflict, they would synthesize, and the thing they were would cease to be. Thus all life was only a becoming, never a being. And all of creation was simply pieces and parts of some great Absolute that was itself becoming.

✳ Cf Schopenhauer

Known as *dialectical materialism*, it and its corollaries were revolutionary ideas that, at the time, lacked any popular audience or influence. Marx's contribution originally was to take Hegel's Absolute and de-spiritualize it, so to speak. He argued that the becoming process had to happen now and not later, on earth and in temporal affairs and not in some state of affairs-yet-to-be. To that end, government or the state becomes the presence of the Absolute on earth, and it is the duty and salvation of every person to serve the state. And to that end, all other forms of authority must be eliminated, principally all notions of god or God and all forms of organized religion. They MUST be stamped out for the state to be supreme, and the state must be supreme for the people to thrive.

Marx would mix this Hegelian heritage with his own theories of economics, publishing in 1867 the first volume of his other, great work, *Das Kapital.* The basic argument here was that those who make and own goods will always be looking for the means by which to make more things more cheaply. At some point, the owner-citizens would succeed so well that they would drive the worker-citizens, on whose backs their economic empires were built, to revolt. Such revolt would destabilize and wreck the state. Such a turn of events must, therefore, at all costs be prevented. Prevention lay in making sure that there never was reason for revolt, and that could only happen if the state removed all means of ownership from individual people and instead owned everything itself in trust for the good of all people.

It is a line of thought that is all too familiar to almost every North American Christian, regardless of his or her age. As an attempt to answer the question of where to place authority, it was a frontal attack not only on religion but also on traditional Reformation concepts about human responsibility, individual worth, and existential purpose. Twenty million people in the Soviet Union alone would be sacrificed on the altar of such thinking before Stalin was done with it.

But there was also a genuine attractiveness to Marx's ideas, and we must be quite clear about that. Good people with bright minds and empowered backgrounds, many of them artists and singers and intellectual leaders, earnestly argued, often to their own social and professional detriment, the virtues of a socialist or a communist state. They argued against the chaos of money-based power and the recurrence of the devastation of worldwide depressions like the Great Depression of 1929. They argued, instead, for the advantages of an authority based on a rational determination of what is best for the most people at any given time and for a kind of proto-secular humanism. This approach, they argued, trumped completely some God-infused, biblically defined code or hierarchy that had been designed for premodern societies. Enlightenment and reason, they said, had set humanity free from ignorance and social vulnerability by furnishing us, instead, with scientifically accurate descriptions of what the cosmos really is and how it works.

An old axiom of folk wisdom holds that one always picks up a bit of whatever it is that one opposes simply by virtue of wrestling with it. As folk wisdom goes, this piece contains an inordinate amount of accuracy. Twentieth-century Christianity in this country met the statism and atheism in communist theory head-on, and American political theory militated from the beginning against the heinous brutality inherent in unfettered power. Nonetheless, we voted in Roosevelt's New Deal and Johnson's Great Society.

Likewise, the midcentury, local church was reconceived as the centralized, hierarchal, and stabilizing organization, the life-giving replacement for, and integration of, all that had been lost when urbanization and automotive mobility ripped us away from a common imagination. Churches began to have more building programs for basketball courts and swimming pools and fellowship halls than for sanctuaries and naves. Hugely expensive to maintain as well as to build, none of those courts and pools and meeting halls had as much to do with spiritual or religious growth in faith as they did with effecting a uniformity of social experience and formation that would be conducive to a uniformity of belief. And the thing to be believed in was a God-infused, biblically sanctioned code of conduct that would have made Jonathan Edwards proud. More to the point, as a code of conduct, it was to be believed in as a means of salvation which, as it turns out, is considerably different from believing in God-among-us as a means of salvation.

The Spiritual Strand and Alcoholics Anonymous

By the 1970s, the young men and women who had been products of all those basketball courts and fellowship halls were rebelling against the burden and the sterility and the disconnect with reality that they constituted. Those children of the late '40s and the '50s who were entering their adulthood would be spiritual, they said, but no longer and never again religious. The first strand in the braid had just been pulled up out of the cable for inspection. It would take almost half a century to finally work it back into place again. But more than just rebellion per se was behind the "I'm spiritual but not religious" mantra.

When speaking of which sociocultural events in the twentieth century most affected North American Christianity and its shifting relationships with spirituality, many sociologists of religion will cite the founding of Alcoholics Anonymous as the first in the list of prime movers. AA officially dates itself, as it should, from 1935 when Bill Wilson and Dr. Bob Smith began to formalize a method of addiction recovery. In actuality, as with Pentecostalism and Azusa Street, so with

AA and 1935. That is, AA also had its precursors, primarily in parts of early twentieth-century evangelicalism like the Oxford Group or Calvary House. It certainly had its roots, to some extent, in the work of William James, whose *Varieties of Religious Experience*, published in 1902, still stands today as one of the early twentieth century's most seminal books. In any event, by 1935 Wilson and Smith had evolved six "principles" or "steps" toward recovery. Shortly thereafter, Wilson would rework the six into smaller units, the result being the now-familiar Twelve Steps of almost every recovery group since.

The informing thing about AA, however, was not so much the Steps themselves as their bases and their implementation. The Steps repeatedly make the point that the addict can be helped only by God . . . not God by the name of Jehovah or El or Adonai or Yahweh or Jesus, but "God as we understand Him." "Choose your own concept of God" was to be one of the early principles that liberated Wilson from his own torment, and he would remain true to it throughout his life. God could even be addressed not as God, but as a/the Higher Power. In fact, health itself seemed to depend upon one's having the power or facility to make just such a leap from the doctrinal to the experiential, and who could effectively argue with that, especially given the increasingly obvious success rate AA was producing?

More than the principle of generic God, which arguably has its popular accession here, AA also assumed from the start that the addicted were better, more effective healers of the addicted than were non-addicted (or non-confessing) experts and authorities, including most particularly pastors and clerics. Now help—effective, productive, demonstrable help—was coming from other, equally wounded and empathetic nonprofessionals. While the American experience was built from the start on anti-clericism, AA and its success, however unintentionally, delivered a serious blow to the role and authority of the clergy, especially Protestant clergy, in this country. That professional standing and influence would receive other, debilitating blows over the rest of the twentieth century, especially during the Civil Rights movement and the Vietnam War; but AA was the first to strike a blow right at the Pastor's Study as the seat of all good advice, holy counsel, wisdom, and amelioration.

Not only did AA, almost by default, begin to supplant the pastoral authority of the professional clergy and open the door to spirituality in the experiencing of a nondoctrinally specific Higher Power, but it also revived the small-group dynamic that would come to characterize later twentieth-century Protestantism and, paradoxically, to enable the disintegration of many of its congregations into pieces and parts. Indeed, so dramatic was the aftereffect of AA's small-group model, some commentators do not even regard it as having had any substantial relation at all to the small-group phenomenon of early Methodism, choosing instead to see AA's approach as being of a different and far more intentional and defined kind. Whatever the case may be, AA opened the floodgates to spirituality by removing the confines of organized religion. The great irony in all of this is that many, many AA groups now meet in church buildings and/or are housed in church-owned property.

Strangers and Countrymen

Even those historians of American religion who commence their commentary on the "spiritual but not religious" phenomenon by citing the advent of AA as its prime enabler, have no problem putting their finger on 1965 as another—or *the* other—great impetus to the burgeoning of free-form spirituality during the latter half of the last century. This was the year in which Congress passed the Immigration and Nationality Services Act.

America, which in its common imagination sees itself as a country of immigrants, has in reality had a very checkered history where immigration policy is concerned. For the closing decades of the nineteenth century, much of the bitterness and furor was over Chinese immigration and the influx of cheap labor that was synonymous with it. During those years, the colorful, railroad barons of the era were trying to outdo one another in laying down the tracks that, by century's end, would connect our East Coast with our West. The problem was that the barons were not laying those tracks with American labor. Indeed not! It was the work-for-next-to-nothing Chinese immigrant who was exploited. And while the barons profited outrageously and the Chinese labored in conditions somewhere between serfdom and outright slavery, it was the average American manual laborer who, caught between the two, starved.

The resulting animus was so vocal and ultimately so violent that Congress in 1882 banned any further immigration of Chinese into this country. Over the years after that, other bills barring entry to all people of Asian descent and/or denying full citizenship to those who were already in the United States were enacted; the United States became almost entirely devoid of Asian influence or perspective; and Pearl Buck's China was as close to any cultural engagement with "the Far East" and its ways as Americans ever got. But then the Second World War came and the Korean War came and, after that, the Vietnam War began its slow march toward disaster, all of them involving Asian theatres of operation, all of them eventuating in person-to-person, human contact between young Americans and the peoples and ways of Asia. Human nature is driven by the imperatives from which it comes, though, and with increasing frequency, the person-to-person contact slipped into romantic love between soldiers and the Asians with whom they wished to spend their lives and by whom they wished to have children. This time the pressure on

Congress was diametrically opposite to that of the previous century. This time the cry was for full freedom of immigration and full access to the privileges and status of citizenship. The 1965 Act granted those very things. It also opened the doors wide to a spirituality that did not require a wrap of religion to function.

Generalizations are dangerous in that they invite the truth of what they say to be destroyed by the inaccuracies or inapplicability of the details that they are generalizing. Nonetheless, generalizations usually have a substantial core of truth in them, as well as provide an economy of observation. The generalization to be made here is that before the coming of the twentieth century, the bulk of American Christianity was word based, rationally argued, and singularly lacking in aesthetic experience. For a rural culture closely entwined with the flow of the natural world and deeply engaged in physical labor, such limitations arguably are of minimal concern. But by the end of the First World War and certainly by the end of the Great Depression, Americans were no longer primarily rural. Instead, they were city dwellers and technology users with that previously unheard of, and very mixed gift of, "free time" or "time on their hands."

A New Religion

The boundary line between free time and boredom is not a clear-cut one; but eventually free time will lead most of us to increasing awareness of our internal experience. The problem for thousands of American Christians—and especially for the American Protestant majority—was that the Christianity they had been born into had given them little or no religion-based vocabulary and few or no religion-based practices or canons by which to articulate, assess, utilize, or interpret this burgeoning world of subjective experience. The words of the more or less new science of psychology were ready to hand, but they were also, by intention, as rational, clinical, sterile, and unsatisfying as they could possibly be. And then came the 1965 Services Act—or more to the point, then came Buddhism.

Then came Buddhism with its rich, rich narrative of wisdom experience, with its centuries of comfortable conversation about the life of the human spirit, with its full vocabulary and lush rhetoric, with its sensible and sensate practices for incorporating the body into the spirit's world, with its exotic ornaments and tranquil aesthetic, with its assurance that worthy and even enviable cultures can arise from meditation as readily as from a frenetic work ethic, with its emphasis on stillness and its teaching about the reality beyond the illusion.

Then came Buddhism with all the tools and appointments needed to enter the subjective experience fully and fearlessly . . . fully, fearlessly, and unencumbered by theism.

The pivot point here is not, per se, the fact that Buddhism, at least in some of its branches, is nontheistic. The pivot point is that, because of its being nontheistic, Buddhism can insinuate itself, quite innocently even, into the practice of almost any institutionalized religion without abrasion or apparent conflict for that religion's faithful. But what happened after 1965 and for two or three decades afterward was much nearer to a wildfire than to infiltration. What happened was that American Christians—and American Jews with them—rushed like the subjectively starving people they were toward the feast of Asian spiritual expertise and experience. Books on how to be a Buddhist Christian or a Buddhist with a proclivity for Christian theology made the country's bestseller lists time and again. Sanghas sprang up, as did Buddhist retreat centers, most of which drew non-Buddhist retreatants in increasing numbers; and *satori* became a buzzword as well as a goal. The gates were indeed now open. The case had been clearly made that the journey of the spirit did not require the baggage of religion to be a worthy and rewarding trek.[3]

The Drug Age

At the same time that Buddhism was opening new worlds to Americans' exploration, so too was the third, great causative agent in this burgeoning of nondoctrinal spirituality. The drug age that came upon us in the 1960s and '70s probably has spawned more human sorrow and waste and wreckage than did any of the century's wars. Yet devastating as that time was and debilitating as its consequences continue to be, the drugs it proffered also proffered a radically different understanding of reality and a radically adjusted perception of subjectivity.

Not only were young America's initial experiments with drugs often approached in religious terms and their results expressed in religious rhetoric, but the vividness of the experience also militated for some deeper, more sophisticated cartography of what the world of the nonphysical was and by whom or what it is inhabited. The barrenness in American culture of Christian teaching about spirituality—and indeed the barrenness of the spirituality that was taught—was equaled only by the stumbling and ineptitude with which an ill-prepared American Protestantism began to try to address the shifting situation. The result was a further exacerbation of "I'm spiritual but not religious" among those who knew to the depths of their interiors that there was more here than the Church had ever told them about. Maybe, even, there was more here than the Church had ever known . . . a possibility very analogous to the repercussions of Columbus's not falling off the flat world of Latin theology, and with much the same disorienting consequences.

While no one wishes to belabor a point, especially in this kind of general survey, we still can not leave the drug era without noting as well that more than any other single thing, drugs opened to public view the question of what is consciousness. As a question, the nature of consciousness certainly, as we have already noted, has long roots in history and strong ones in the work of nineteenth-century medicine and pure science, but it has its first stentorian cry of full birthing here. There is a clear trajectory from Timothy Leary straight to the Great Emergence and our current disorientation about what exactly consciousness is and we are.

The Erosion of *Sola Scriptura*

When we look at the question of consciousness in terms of the drug revolution, we obviously are revisiting one of our secondary questions, this time in terms more of the experiential and immediate than of the theoretical. We need to stop a moment and do the same thing now with our overarching question of authority, and for the same reasons.

As we know, *sola scriptura, scriptura sola* had answered the authority question in the sixteenth century and, more or less, had sustained the centuries between the Great Reformation and the latter half of the nineteenth century when the seeds of the Great Emergence were being planted. But there was—and still is—another, ongoing chain of experiential events that leads inexorably from the nineteenth century straight to the disestablishment of "only Scripture and Scripture only" in American Christian belief.

The first such blow to Luther's resolution of the authority question came in this country with the Civil War and the years preceding it. While the Bible does not order up slavery as a practice to be followed by the faithful, it certainly does acknowledge it as an institution. And while it does not sanction slavery, it likewise nowhere condemns it. We do ourselves and our understanding of our forebears a great disservice if we do not acknowledge the fact that on the very basis of this biblical ambivalence, thousands and thousands of godly and devout Christians fought for the practice of slavery as being biblically permitted and accepted. No one presumably is naive enough to think that the War Between the States did not have huge cultural and economic factors at work in every heated debate that preceded the outbreak of war. It is equally naive and redactionist, however, to ignore the fact that America's Protestant churches almost all split in two, violently and on theological grounds, over the issue of scriptural teachings about slavery. Those agonized cries on both sides of the divide have to be remembered now for what they were: the fearsome cries of those for whom the undergirding of "Scripture only and only Scripture" had been, if not ripped asunder, then most certainly set atilt.

Because the business of one person's owning another person is neither morally defensible nor economically sensible in an industrialized society, we got over this major blow to *sola scriptura*. It was a slow and sometimes exquisitely painful recovery, but we did recover, until the Great War rattled our bars again, this time over gender instead of race. Although we may argue with some success that the Garden of Eden does not really make woman subject to man, it is impossible to argue that St. Paul does not operate from that principle. Yet now, in this new century, American women were demanding with increased ferocity their equal enfranchisement in American life and politics. This clearly was a violation of the Bible's way! . . . Well, it may have been, but the truth was that the biblical way simply could not stand up to the grinding, day-by-day onslaught of domestic pressure. In a relatively short time, women got the vote, and men got their suppers hot and on time again. It was hardly a religious solution, but nonetheless it was a very welcome one.

By midcentury, a far more intractable question had arisen, however; that of divorce. There is almost no way to revisit the divorce debates without unearthing personal stories of the abuses and horrors that led, ultimately, to its acceptance into American Christianity. Every family has its tales about the great-aunt who was beaten routinely by her husband or the family reduced to chronic illness and malnutrition by an alcoholic householder or the distant cousin that was repeatedly abused sexually because the non-offending parent could neither control the situation nor find faithful means to escape it.

In all truth, we must acknowledge that what the Bible actually says about divorce is not quite so black-and-white or unbending as were the Church's teachings on the subject. That distinction either was not seen at the time, however, or else it was seen by the average preacher as only a fine line which it was very dangerous to cross. But in time divorce came anyway, leaving in its wake the inevitable and predictable carnage of family instability and too easy an escape from the problems of shared living. And leaving in its wake as well another—and this time more intimate and personal—blow to *sola scriptura*. Now the Church was accepting what clearly it had taught against for centuries. Beyond that, and even more discouraging or debilitating, was the fact that before century's end, the Church would be accepting divorced clergy as not only professionally able but also morally uncompromised.

The next assault in this progression of assaults was the ordination of women to the Protestant clergy. Here it is indeed impossible to wiggle around the scripturally recorded edict that a woman must keep quiet in the assembly. If she has questions, St. Paul says, she is to ask them of her husband later and at home. This time there was not, and could never be, any question of alternative interpretations or variant translations or Jewish practices that had been rendered obsolete by Christianity's coming.

The ordination of women was followed, of course, by their elevation to the episcopacy in the Episcopal Church in the United States. Clearly the battle of "Scripture only" was being lost. Now there was only one more tool left in *sola scriptura*'s war chest. There was only one more pawn left on the board, only one more puck on the playing field. Enter "the gay issue."

To approach any of the arguments and questions surrounding homosexuality in the closing years of the twentieth century and the opening ones of the twenty-first is to approach a battle to the death. When it is all resolved—and it most surely will be—the Reformation's understanding of Scripture as it had been taught by Protestantism for almost five centuries will be dead. That is not to say that Scripture as the base of authority is dead. Rather it is to say that what the Protestant tradition has taught about the nature of that authority will be either dead or in mortal need of reconfiguration. And that kind of summation is agonizing for the surrounding culture in general. In particular, it is agonizing for the individual lives that have been built upon it. Such an ending is to be staved off with every means available and resisted with every bit of energy that can be mustered. Of all the fights, the gay one must be—has to be—the bitterest, because once it is lost, there are no more fights to be had. It is finished. Where now is the authority?

The Corporeal Strand

Before we leave this particular line of thought, however, we need to note one more thing of significance about the progression of assaults on Protestantism's interpretation of Scripture as sole authority. While the erosion of *sola scriptura* is clearly an erosion of the base of traditional, denominational Protestantism's authority, we must remember that it is a corporeal, not a spiritual or moral, issue. It is part of the second strand of the interior braid in our cable of meaning. That is, because Protestantism planted its standard dead center of a biblical absolutism without mercy or malleability, it planted itself in doctrine, in a codified set of beliefs that must be adhered to. Protestants are and always have been "believers," one's beliefs becoming one's self-definition of what "Christian" is. Defined as a codified set of beliefs, doctrine, once it exists, is by definition proof positive that an institutionalized form of religion exists. It is proof positive that a set of religious sensibilities has now assumed body and form and power. It is corporeal.

Our North American fingering of the second or corporeal strand in the braid has been going on for decades, of course, in more ways than changes in social mores. Most commonly, it has presented itself as dissension over a proposed new hymnal or a translation of Holy Writ that differs in some way from that of previous decades or a reintroduction of ancient practices more associated in the popular mind with Latin Christianity than with Early Church Christianity. Raucous as some of those scrimmages have been, they have lacked the trans-denominational ferocity of the race/gender/sexual preference progression. They were not, in other words, fights that jumped a communion's walls to involve the surrounding, general culture. The fact that race/gender/sexual preference have jumped the barriers and become cultural fights means that we may be nearing the end of our absorption with the corporeal strand; we may be almost ready to think about stuffing it, like spirituality, snugly back into the braid so that we can begin to focus ever so loudly on morality.

The Moral Strand

Our re-formation absorption or fascination with morality—with the third strand in the cable's braid—is usually presented as having begun to rear its head with *Roe v. Wade* and the abortion issue. As an interpretive position, that one is arguable. That is, the protesting pro-lifers generally claim the doctrinal position of biblical literacy as the basis for their stance. "Thou shalt not kill" and "Let the little children come unto me" are indeed clearly biblical, as well as pertinent, citations. On the other hand, what allows the argument (and what will block its resolution for many years) is a moral, rather than a doctrinal, issue. That issue is the distinctly emergent, definitively second-tier, question of what is and is not a human being. Is a morula a human being or a product of conception? Does a blastula know itself? Does an embryo? A fetus? When? And is knowing self a definition of life? Is the perception of pain, life? By what standard of assessment? And so on and so forth.

Where one chooses to position the pro-life/pro-choice debate does not change the fact, however, that since April 2005, we, as a culture in re-formation, have been deeply preoccupied with fingering the third strand of the braid. Terri Schiavo died in April of that year; and the months running up to her death and those running down from it since have been ones of distinctly moral debate. "Thou shalt not kill" still appertains, but to permit death is not the same as to inflict it. And the distinction between *permit* and *inflict* lies inexorably buried in the question of what is human consciousness and/or consciousness's relation to humanness.

Almost as much to the point is the fact that mercy is too fluid a concept to be doctrinalized. Yet, it is theories of mercy that shape and inform the morality of *permit*. We have sensed this for quite some time now, of course. As a people, we were first flummoxed by it well before the Schiavo case, in the public furor that attended Dr. Jack Kevorkian. The problem is that, all these years later, we still have not conceptualized an ethos based on it. Generally accepted principles of morality are a work in progress for emergence culture, in other words. Presumably, they will be for quite some time yet.

Technological Advances

Time and space will hardly permit the elaboration of some of the three-dozen-plus other social, technological, political, and cultural changes that rose up in the peri-Emergence of the twentieth century. Certainly, before we leave this part of our discussion, though, we need to acknowledge just a few of them, even if we do so with no more than a brief mention.

We need to remind ourselves, for instance, of two things we already know: first, the religious expression or result of the Great Emergence is a new configuration of Christianity, and second, this new "emerging" or "emergent" Christianity is fundamentally a body of people, a conversation, if you will. Only after that does it become a corpus of solutions and characteristics, accommodations and principles. It is a conversation being conducted, moreover, by people from diverse cultures and points of reference, as well as from widely divergent Christian backgrounds.

As we will soon see, approximately one quarter of today's "emergents" and "emergings" are Roman Catholic, not Protestant, in background and natal formation. For that reason, any treatment of the peri-Emergence must acknowledge the presence and enormous, formative impact of both Vatican I and Vatican II on Roman Catholicism in particular and on re-traditioning and emergent/emerging Christianity in general.

Vatican I, convoked in 1869, technically did not end until 1960, when Pope John XXIII formally closed it in order to make way for Vatican II in 1962. The two councils, which have been the basis of innumerable volumes in and of themselves, anticipated, as Protestantism did not, the central questions of the new re-formation. In effect, they did much of the original spade work or heavy lifting, so to speak, in that they attempted to forestall the questions by answering them before they could be fully articulated in the communion at large.

While Vatican I most famously dealt with the authority issue by establishing the principle of Papal Infallibility as dogma, it also dealt extensively with Latin understanding of Scripture and its applications, origins, and role. Vatican II, which is more familiar to most Americans, was a course correction of another sort. That is, it sought to ameliorate much of the Church's traditionalist reaction to modernism; but it was also deeply engaged with the issues surrounding ecumenism, interfaith dialogue, and the formulation of an acceptable theology of religion. Regardless of what form or forms of Christianity may rise up out of the Great Emergence, in other words, it is safe to say that much of the thinking and many of the effectual conclusions will have had their initial roots in the Vatican Councils.

We need, certainly, to recognize here the impact of medical advances and how they drastically changed the form and nature of perceived human vulnerability and, as a result, the popular understanding of exactly what the role of the Church and/or its clergy was and is in healing. Second, those very advances, with their greater skills in defeating disease and staving off death, have eventuated, obviously, in questions exactly like the Schiavo and Kevorkian ones. Less flamboyant and far less theoretical and distant, however, are the questions they have evoked about routine geriatric treatment and end-of-life intervention, its morality, its imperatives, its costs, and its standards.

We must recognize that the coming of individually programmed technologies like the Sony Walkman or the iPod or the programmable cell phone made superb music not only accessible outside of churches and concert halls, but also made it highly participatory. One has only to watch folk, their ears soundly plugged, walking down the street with their fingers clicking, their feet jazzing, and their eyes half closed to understand why performed music coming from ordinary organs to seated audiences in meetinghouse sanctuaries lacks a certain immediacy and/or street appeal. Perhaps no other single thing has so threatened and changed the hegemony of formal Christian worship as has this shift in our general affection from performed to participatory music.

We can not ignore the fact that computer science has unleashed upon us nanotechnology and artificial intelligence and concepts like the Singularity with all their concomitant legal, moral, and religious questions. The problem inherent in all of them is that we are a public whose extant religious institutions have to date shown themselves to be ill-prepared both theologically and intellectually to wrestle with the practical implications involved in such intellectual and technological developments.

We must acknowledge as well that the world has indeed gone flat again, the Reformation's nation-state having given way to the Emergence's globalization. Cash, which replaced blood as the basis of power during the peri-Reformation, now has had to cede power over to sheer information in the Emergence. And to some greater or lesser extent, every social or political unit is in thrall to those who know the most about how to destroy the most or expedite the most, whether such threatening agents be next door or three continents away.

We can not ignore the passing of much religious experience, instruction, and formal worship from sacred space to secular space and, perhaps even more significantly, into electronic space. The progression from the radio preachers of the first half of the twentieth century to the television "sermons" or visits of Bishop Fulton Sheen in the midcentury to the televangelists of the later half of the century to the churches and worship sites of the Internet is an uninterrupted movement to a more and more interiorized or imaged religious praxis. Millions of Americans now receive their entire pastoral care and have their whole religious instruction and engagement on the Internet through websites ranging from the sociability of worship in Second Life to the prayerful quiet of gratefulness.org to the informational and formative offerings of sites like beliefnet.com.

Nor can we, in speaking of the computer and cyberspace, forget that both have connected each of us to all the rest of us. The hierarchal arrangement or structure of most extant Churches and denominations is based on the hierarchal arrangement of the Reformation's evolving nation-states. It is, however, quite alien and suspect, if not outright abhorrent, to second-generation citizens of cyberspace where networking and open- or crowd-sourcing are more logical and considerably more comfortable. In our connectedness, of course, we also experience with immediacy the pain and agony, incongruities and horrors, of life as it is lived globally, forcing the question of theodicy to take on a kind of total-humanity angst or urgency that has not accrued since the Black Death leveled the earth five and six centuries ago. The rise of aggressive atheism in the opening decade of the twenty-first century, in fact, finds much of its explanation and raison d'être in this very fact.

It has been said over and over again—and quite correctly—that the Reformation's cry of *sola scriptura* was accompanied and supported by the doctrine of the priesthood of all believers. The computer, opening up as it does, the whole of humankind's bank of collective information, enables the priesthood of all believers in ways the Reformation could never have envisioned. It also, however, opens up all that information to anybody, but without the traditional restraints of vetting or jurying; without the controls of informed, credentialed access; and without the accompaniment or grace of mentoring. It even opens up with equal élan the world's bank of dis-information. To the extent that faith can be formed or dissuaded by the contents of the mind as well as those of the heart, then such license has huge implications for the Great Emergence and for what it will decide to do about factuality in a wiki world.

Rosie the Riveter

But before we conclude our overview of how the Great Emergence came to be, and of the more obvious events of the twentieth century that have shaped emergents themselves, we need to look in detail at one last chain of circumstances. At first blush, this one may seem as peripheral as did our discussion of the coming of the Model T (to which it is, by the way, related). In reality, though, like the coming of the family automobile, this string of changes has worked in concert with the rest of the twentieth century to create what arguably may be one of the most informing elements of them all.

Her name was Rosie—Rosie the Riveter—and she was born in 1941. That was the year that the gathering storm of World War II broke forth in all its fury, and there was no more accommodation. America was at war, the irony being that we had next to nothing with which to fight a war. Our tanks and guns and ships were all antiques wrapped in mothballs or else they were the property of Japan, to whom we had sold them some years before simply as a means of getting rid of them all. The First World War had, after all, been the war to end war . . . in theory, that is.

When war was declared, soldiers were mustered up and conscription was begun, the result being that over the next five years almost every able-bodied American male was on active military duty. We affectionately called him/them "Johnny" and prayed for safety now and peace soon. But Johnny had nothing with which to protect himself and very little with which to fight his way toward peace. Johnny did, however, have a wife. We, within a matter of months, came to call her Rosie; and the years would make of her one of America's most loved and honored icons.

The traditional family, the so-called nuclear family that the peri-Reformation created and Protestantism enshrined, was, as we all know, hierarchal. The male head-of-house was the unit's chief defender, provider, and director. Second in command was "his" wife whose area of influence and responsibility was domestic primarily, and social only secondarily, if at all. The children were the plebes of the family, but there was no question that in most cases, it was for them and their furtherance that the family existed. The father's economic and managerial efforts and the mother's domestic ones were directed toward the support and maintenance of the home.

When war came, however, and all the Johnnies went off empty-handed to fight, the American government turned to the only workforce still available to us. We turned to Rosie. And to get Johnny safely home and to assure that their children would never live under an alien regime, America's women responded. Young and middle-aged women who had never worked for pay in their lives, much less outside of their own homes, took their little ones down the street to Grandma's house or Aunt Susie's, then rolled up their sleeves, punched in their time cards, and went to work throwing the rivets that made the planes that made America and home safe again.[4]

By any name, what America's women of the 1940s did was an amazement. Women, made strong by years of hoeing gardens, toting wet laundry, chopping stove wood, and riding herd on children, took their mechanical and economic naiveté in hand and assumed the very same jobs that their husbands had always said were unladylike, not fitting, too arduous. If one listens to the Rosies of World War II, however, if one reads their memoirs and letters, one finds not the faintest whiff of feminism. If there is pride here—and there is—it is pride in a job well done for the sake of protecting what was and is.

Certainly there was a paycheck. It was needed, because Johnny's army pay was hardly equal to the routine costs of caring for a house and children. If there was a shifting about in the nature and range of social contact, then that was only coincidental to the business of throwing rivets. If there were a certain subtle easing of stress when there was no director other than one's self to determine domestic policy and decisions, then it was embraced as compensatory, not as a pleasure to be desired forever. If there were a kind of unnatural

109

relief in being able to hand one's children off to others for much of the day and sometimes even for a night or two, then weariness and duty overwhelmed any luxuriating in some sense of false freedom.

Before the war's end, over twenty million American women would be gainfully employed in defense work. Once the war was over, though, and once the men were home, most of those women went back quite willingly, even gratefully, to the domestic role they had originally been reared to fulfill. There were two or three problems, however, with that resumption of business-as-once-it-had-been. The first was the kind of restiveness that attends when one has seen a wider world and then is returned to a more socially, fiscally, and potentially restricted one. Perhaps not an expressed or even an explosive problem, that restiveness was nonetheless an erosive one.

The second problem was that with war and the increasing sophistication required to win it had come such technology as the world never before had known. There was little or no chopping of stove wood to occupy an hour a day and considerable amounts of energy. The stove in the kitchen worked on switches, and the heat came from an automatic furnace in the basement. There were no more dirty clothes to scrub on the scrub board, and no more wet laundry to tote outside and hang on the line. One machine did the washing, and six inches away was the matching machine that did the drying. Sweeping and mopping gave way to vacuuming. In fact, Mrs. Johnny found her gender-assigned work strangely lacking in physical outlets or logistical challenges. She also found herself possessed of hours of time and little notion of exactly what to do with them.

The third problem was that the children whose fathers had left for war and come back again, whose mothers had worked the factories and manned, quite literally, the war effort, remembered a different domestic structure and a different set of domestic politics. They remembered, and their notions of home had been shaped by, five years when the rules had been different. They remembered when Mama had been somebody, when her picture—or the picture of some other lady just like her—had been plastered on walls and public buildings all over town as evidence of the best of America and the American spirit. Some of them—a lot of them, perhaps—remembered when there had been no fights after lights-out, when harsh words overheard had not threatened one's sense of safety and stability. Some of them undoubtedly remembered a time when mama had had money to share or even, occasionally, to spend on her own fancy.

At the risk of once again generalizing too much, it is still true that the stereotypical or average Rosie took care of her restiveness by increasing her social life via the telephone and the nearest church. The church, in fact, became for her and many of her kind the solution of choice for that second problem of freed or empty time. The midcentury church could invent programs faster than their women congregants could man them; and busy is, if not good, then at least sedative. In effect, Rosie morphed into June Cleaver, and Johnny morphed into Ward. Beaver, being a boy, was the cliché of national choice for all the happy children in post–World War II, proper, American, Christian society.

The pity was that Beaver had a brother, Wally, but no sister. Had she existed, however, she might have left us some kind of archival record of how she got from being June's little girl to being one of Betty Friedan's groupies. The third problem, in other words, was one neither Rosie nor Johnny could fix. The memory—the actual, lived knowledge—of another way of being female was ingrained in the heads and hearts of thousands of young women who had been born under the original model, been reared in the amended one, and been returned in the heat of adolescence to the original one.

They had no catchy name, those young women who had seen a different way of being female; but they had fury and intention. Never,

111

never would they be the submissive wives their mothers had begun as and returned to. They would riot and defy, but they would also get themselves college educations and teach themselves and each other financial acumen. They would break the old rules and live in freedom with a man, but without the entanglement of legal indenture or the liability of common finances. They would work harder than men, if that's what it took, but they would, at whatever cost, be respected as equal, not secondary, citizens.

The world had pivoted.

Family Reconfigured

Re-formations do indeed always have the requirement of answering anew the question of the proper location and definition of authority. They likewise always have one or two subsidiary questions like the ones for the Great Emergence of a theology of religion and the definition of what "human" is and what consciousness is and does. There just may be, however, a third subsidiary question for this re-formation of ours, though ours will not be the first upheaval in which it has reared its head. The third question is, "What now is society's basic or foundational unit?"

For five hundred years, the nuclear family was the established unit upon which the larger society was itself established. In this country alone, for over three centuries, everything from our legal codes and political proselytizing to our religious propaganda and church programming assumed and rested upon that unit with its traditional deployment of responsibilities and its unquestioned chain of command. When the country preacher of mid-twentieth-century America decried divorce as a threat "right at the heart of America," he was neither in error nor benighted. He may not have been arguing from religious conviction so much as from his own private unease about what a Pandora's box there was for the status quo at the end of that road; but he was still right.

When, in the same two or three decades, not only divorce, but Rosie came upon us, there was no turning back, except for one small thing. True equality of the sexes in opportunity and public power would forever be limited, or so the common wisdom held, so long as women were emotionally and physically compromised by monthly menses and by pregnancy. Those fundamental functions of biology would hold forever, and forever guarantee at least some periods of vulnerability when the male's natural strength and protective aggression would be necessary and appreciated. And that would have been true had 1960 not come upon us and, with it, the release to general use by the Food and Drug Administration of the birth control pill.

It slipped up on us, so to speak. Greeted first with curiosity, then with tentative acceptance, and within two or three years hailed as God's gift to the overly fertile, the pill soon thereafter became God's gift to emancipation, God's tool for total equality. The playing field was now level in a way that even legal divorce could never have made it.

"An important meeting is coming up at the office next Friday, and I must be at my very best, but my period is due on Wednesday. I can't afford the distraction or the dullness of menstruation, so I'll just take an extra day or two of pills. It won't hurt anything, and nobody will be the wiser," Rosie's daughter says to herself. And she, too, is right. It did not hurt anything, and it did ensure that she was at the top of her game. And by the turn of the twenty-first century, not only would the American woman have changed, but so also would the pill. By the turn of the century, the science behind the pill would have advanced enough so that not only could America's women delay childbearing for as long as they wished, but they could also completely block menses for years without any obvious detriment.

There is, again, nothing inherently right or wrong in these changes. There is only change itself. What change meant, in this scenario, was that now the average husband and wife were, first, a two-income family. Increasingly, those incomes were close to equivalent; sometimes they were even disproportionate in favor of the woman's wages. Because money is power, money—a salary check of her own—is also freedom; or it is a ready-to-hand ticket to freedom should the present arrangement cease to be acceptable for some reason or other.

Additionally, both marriage partners, for the first time in American history, were receiving not only their fiscal but also their psychological income and rewards from sources external to their family unit. And for perhaps the first time in human history, the home—the physical place and the children and relationships that were in it—was not what work was first and foremost about. Once upon a time, the father had gone forth to conquer the world only so he could bring the world, or at least a portion of it, home as trophy and enabling means for the family. Once upon a time, the mother had been there always to soothe and appreciate the father and to create the home for which he worked. Now both went forth to conquer the world. In doing so, they had to "make arrangements for child care," which usually meant that one or another of them also had to pick up weary children on the way home from work. And home? Why, home was no more the reason for work. It was instead the place where all the members of the family came to regroup and regain the energy required to go back out there and conquer again.

With the automobile, as we have noted, we lost some of the conservatory influence of the traditional matriarch. With the acceptability of divorce, with the Rosie years of World War II and their aftermath, and finally with the coming of the pill, we lost the traditional mother, and with her going, we lost the traditional or nuclear family. Census figures, early in the twenty-first century, predictably enough, were already showing declining birth rates among women of European descent and an advancing age, across the board, for first pregnancies. But they were also reporting for the first time in our history that just barely—by a slim point or two, but still irrefutably—more Americans lived in nontraditional family structures than traditional ones. Slightly more of us, in other words, lived alone or out of wedlock or in extended families or with affinity groups than lived in households composed of married partners of the opposite sex rearing the biological or adopted children of their union. Where now—or what now—is the basis for our social order?

While we do not presently know the answer to that question (though there are some intriguing and educated guesses moiling about), we do know one of the more obvious problems that has arisen from our lack of, if not an answer, a temporary fix. The most obvious is—and has been for three or four decades—that once the female is occupied outside the home for a full working day, she suffers the same physical and mental exhaustion as does the male. What that translates to is the complete reorientation of the evening hours in the family's life. The solidifying bond of a shared meal is often sacrificed, certainly, but more to the point for the Christianity of the Great Emergence, so too are the traditional time of family-based religious instruction and formation.

Scripture's Place

When World War II broke out, the average American youngster, whether Protestant or Roman Catholic, was possessed of a reasonable familiarity with Bible stories and a formative grasp of the religious and moral points contained in them. Most of that sub-rosa information had been instilled at home in dinner conversations, family altars, Bible-story reading, and bedtime prayers. Biblical literacy and cultural literacy were totally entwined, one with the other, as was biblical and familial instruction. When the mother as principal storyteller and domestic rabbi ceased, bit by bit, to function in those roles, America's younger generations became more and more untethered from the parables and prophecies, interpretations and principles that supported both the story itself and the consensual illusion that was based on it.[5]

The result, theologically, for both emergent Christianity and the reactive bodies of American Protestantism and American Roman Catholicism is stark. Each one of them, in dealing with Americans under fifty, is dealing in large measure with scriptural innocents whose very ignorance is pushing them in one of two directions. Either innocence of scriptural experience is propelling them to seek ever more eagerly for structured engagement with it, or else a total lack of prior exposure is propelling Scripture itself farther and farther into the attics of life where all antiques are stored for a respectful period of time before being thrown completely away. Which extreme is worse is hard to say, for naifs of every kind are vulnerable at every turn . . . easily exploited, easily crippled, easily sacrificed.

But enough of such overviews, listings, and history. It is time to turn our attention at last to the more immediate present and to our near future. It is time to answer our final question: Where is this thing going, even as it is carrying all of us along with it in its mad career?

---

1. There is perhaps no more accessible or informative treatment of the cultural impact of Heisenberg's physics than David Lindley's *Uncertainty— Einstein, Heisenberg, Bohr, and the Struggle for the Soul of Science* (Doubleday, 2007). It should be required reading for every North American Christian who wants to grasp fully what the Great Emergence stands in juxtaposition to.

2. In general, Charismatic Christians, whose form of belief and worship came up out of Pentecostalism, do not like to be placed in the same category, or even the same sentence, with those from whom they have separated. In respect for that concern, but in recognition of the fact that the similarities are greater than the differences in terms of ecclesial implications, the Pew Foundation in 2006 began to refer to both bodies under the overarching name of "Renewalists," a title which we will use throughout the rest of this volume.

3 The advent of Buddhism into popular culture had been preceded by the introduction into this country of Theosophy and the work of Madame Helene Blavatsky. Theosophy, which never commanded the general imagination, drew heavily on Eastern theory and particularly on Hindu thought. Despite the fact that it was "spiritual," it nonetheless organized itself and conceived of itself as a religion. Because its adherents were often men and women of high intellectual, cultural, and/or social standing, however, the principles of Theosophy enjoyed a cachet of respectability that in turn helped break ground for myriad strands of Eastern thought and, many observers would say, even for the New Age and Age of Aquarius excitement of popular spirituality during the latter half of the twentieth century.

4. In point of fact, there were as many or more welded seams on gunboats as there were riveted ones on planes; and briefly we called Mrs. Johnny by the name of Wendy the Welder. The drama of throwing rivets triumphed, however, and Wendy lost pride of place to Rosie in our patriotic affections.

5. Those who wish to explore this point and its implications in greater detail can find a feast of information and insight in *Religious Literacy: What Every American Needs to Know* by Stephen Prothero (HarperOne, 2007).

PART 3

THE
Great
EMERGENCE

Where Is It Going?

There is a certain temerity, if not outright arrogance, in thinking that any of us can answer before the fact such a question as where a cataclysmic shift in human affairs ultimately is going to go. There is an equal foolheartedness, however, in not trying to discern the near future of our lives, both as citizens of a polity in upheaval and as believers in an organized religion that concomitantly is in upheaval as a result. So answer the question we must. But to answer it with as great an accuracy as we can muster, we need first to remind ourselves of the restrictions laid upon this conversation.

The Great Emergence, like the Great Reformation or the Great Schism or the time of the Great Gregory or the Great Transformation, is a generalized social/political/economic/intellectual/cultural shift. Like its predecessors, this one too is a phenomenon initiating in the Western experience; though unlike the preceding reconfigurations, the Great Emergence is not limited to the Western world in its expectations, expression, or exercise. It suffers also from an unfortunate confusion of terms that its predecessors did not have to surmount.

The Great Reformation was clearly a historical period that, in resolving itself, eventuated in the hegemony of a new form of Christianity bearing the distinct and distinguishing name of "Protestantism." This time around, the Great Emergence has given rise to a form of Christianity called, not apart from itself, but rather after itself. The result is an all-too-ready intermingling of context with content and vice versa. That is, we use the term the "Great Emergence" to name a movement within Christianity as easily and as often as we use it to name the larger context in which the shift in Christianity is occurring and to which it is responding. The result is that to engage in any meaningful discussion of "The Great Emergence," one must be very clear about which part of the thing one is trying to describe. In the instance here and for the rest of this conversation, unless otherwise indicated, we are talking about the Great Emergence in terms of its religious integrity or presentations.

We are also talking here about the Great Emergence in terms of emergent or emerging Christianity while, at the same time, being very mindful that first-world Judaism is undergoing shifts and accommodations more or less analogous to those occurring in Christianity. We must likewise remind ourselves again that we are looking at emergent and emerging Christianity from the North American, and primarily the United States, perspective. Yet emergent Christianity in this country does not exist in isolation, either geographically or culturally.

The United Kingdom, Australia, New Zealand, Europe, and several parts of Africa and Asia are experiencing shifts in Christian thinking and sensibilities similar to those we are undergoing. More to the point, emergence in the UK was clearly active, discernible, and describable at least twenty years before it was nearly so visible and coherent in this country, making observation of what is happening in England, Ireland, and Wales a very useful and sometimes predictive exercise for North American observers. Even more to the point is the fact that the major leaders and strategists of the Great Emergence in this country are engaging more and more intentionally in ongoing exchanges between themselves and emergent leaders outside of the US. This intentionality has had the additional benison of allowing emergents from cohorts outside the United States to influence and participate in what is happening in North American Christianity.

One of the hallmarks of the Church's semi-millennial rummage sales has always been that when each of the things was over and the dust had died down, Christianity would not only have readjusted itself, but it would also have grown and spread. Never has that principle been more operative than now. In the hands of emergents, Christianity has grown exponentially, not only in geographic base and numbers, but also in passion and in an effecting belief in the Christian call to the brotherhood of all peoples.

Given all of these things, what now can be said of this new configuration of Christianity that is taking us in North America, lock, stock, and church door, to some other way of living out our faith in an equally reconfigured secular context? Several things, in fact, the first of which is to say that we have a fairly clear understanding now of the currents on which we are riding. We have a fairly clear picture, in other words, of what emergent Christianity is made up of and of why and how its constituent parts have come together to form a new whole.

6

The Gathering Center

And the Many Faces of a Church Emerging

Stories about the evolution of the Great Transformation are, as a rule, fairly skeletal, but they do include one of singular interest to us here. They include the history and naming of that moment and place where what had been a variant or new form of Abrahamic religion became so distinct and other as to merit a new name peculiar unto itself. The story of that dramatic shift, recorded in the Book of the Acts, chapter 11, chronicles the gradual concentration, over a period of several months, of reconfiguring Cypriots and Cyreneans in the city of Antioch. As their numbers and enthusiasm grew, they in essence rose to the pitch of outright foment, calling first Barnabas and then Paul to come and minister to them. And it was in that place and within the time of that foment, we are told, that the newly reconfigured believers were first called Christian. It was at that point that this new thing—this new way of being faithful in a new world—

became so clearly distinct from what had been as to be worthy of a name of its own.

In the same way, while it is difficult, if not impossible, to select any one event or date in the fourteenth century as being the tipping point that slid Europe over into the Great Reformation, we do know when and where those tensions gave birth to the form of Christianity we now know as Protestantism. Or at least we know something analogous to that. We know that the original *Protestatio*, from which the new way of being derived its name, was drawn up only twelve years after Luther wrote his 95 Theses. In February of that year, 1529, the Diet of Speyer met and passed legislation that, in essence, denied freedom of religious exercise in any form other than that of Roman Catholicism and declared an end to toleration of any deviations from the established form of Latin Christianity. Two months later, in April, five "re-forming" princes and fourteen cities of the Holy Roman Empire, feeling themselves compelled by God to speak their new truth, signed a *Protestatio* and, in so doing, gave their new form of Christianity its name. Such has not been the case with the Great Emergence.

There is simply no grand framing story or even unanimity of opinion yet about when precisely it was that this new thing—this new, emerging way of being Christian in an emerging new world—became so clearly distinct from what had been as to be worthy of a name of its own. None of us can, with confidence, look back over the closing years of the twentieth century and say, "Here . . . just here . . . is when we can see enough of the thing to declare that it is actively here and distinctly separate from all that has previously been." We can, however, trace some of the course of its coming by looking at what religion scholars and historians observed and wrote during that century of emergence's early formation in North America.

Perhaps the first prominent American scholar actually to perceive what was happening and then write about it in some detail was

Walter Rauschenbusch. As early as 1907, Rauschenbusch declared that Western humanity was "in the midst of a revolutionary epoch fully as thorough as that of the Renaissance and Reformation" and predicted an approaching crisis for the Church as well as the society in which it existed.[1]

By midcentury, we find observers like Paul Tillich speaking in letters and conversation about shifting times and shifting foundations; and by the mid to late-sixties, matters had become even clearer. Before the decade's end, scholars had begun not only to speak about and describe what was happening but also to predict what probably was going to happen. World War II was over, Hiroshima and the Holocaust were facts, Korea and the Berlin Wall were raw memories in a tense world, the Drug Age was upon us, Mainline Protestantism was just beginning to wither a bit, the Jesus Freaks were bizarre as well as faintly worrisome, Vietnam was everywhere and always in our faces . . . the world had wobbled entirely free of its axis, and all things were at last in full upheaval.

Sketching the Church

By the end of the 1960s, historians, theologians, and observers were also beginning to define the times and predict the coming decades in terms of a new paradigm that they could, and did, begin to sketch out in diagram form. What they were doing by the late 1960s was tentative at first and looked something like the following illustration.

Called a *quadrilateral*, the assessment was that by the turn of the century North American Christianity (including all its extant forms) would be divided into four, roughly equal groups or categories like those shown below.[2] The quadrilateral shown here is different in a point or two from earlier ones circulating in the late 1960s, however. Originally, for instance, the term "Liturgicals" in the left

The Quadrilateral

Liturgicals	Social Justice Christians
Renewalists	Conservatives

upper quadrant was assumed to mean, at a practical, working level, only Roman Catholics and Anglicans, along with a few Lutheran congregations of a more liturgical bent. There was, at that time, so small a presence in North America of either Oriental or Eastern Orthodoxy as to make inclusion of those bodies in broad overviews superfluous. That is no longer true, and the reader should assume the presence of the Orthodox as now being very much a part of the Liturgical quadrant.

Originally, commentators called the upper right box by the name of "Mainline" Christians. Today that term not only has no real meaning, but it also carries a certain erroneous cachet of morbidity in popular conversation. Instead, it is now more customary to use the term, as here, "Social Justice" Christians.

As we noticed earlier, the term "Renewalists" in the lower left box is of more recent coinage and means to include both Charismatic and Pentecostal Christians under one rubric. The last box—the lower right one—is the difficult one. At one point, it was labeled "Fundamentalists," but if "Mainline" bears an unfortunate cachet in the public conversation, "Fundamentalist" bears a downright odoriferous one. The name for this fourth quadrant has accordingly shifted time and time again over the years from "Evangelicals" to "Theocrats" to "Conservatives" and back again. For the time being, the latter title of "Conservatives" seems the more inclusive and most neutral label.

Not included here are two significant bodies—Mormons and Quakers. Mormonism, which is growing rapidly domestically and globally, is arguably the fourth of the great Abrahamic faiths rather than a subset or variant of Christianity and increasingly is so treated by religionists. Accordingly, it is omitted here. The omission of the Quakers is a temporary, narrative convenience rather than an omission as such. We will touch on their considerable contribution to, and unique place in, the Great Emergence in due time.

Changing Shapes

In considering this initial diagram, the temptation is to do as we have just done and think of each box in terms of the strands or denominations that fall within it—Roman Catholics within the Liturgical quadrant, Methodists in the Social Justice box, Southern Baptists in the Conservative one, Assemblies of God in the Renewalists quadrant, etc. There was a time—fifty, forty, even perhaps thirty years ago—when each denomination or communion in North American Christendom was internally consistent and cohesive enough for that sort of parsing to be, if not ideal, at least not incorrect. Such ceased to be the case at least fifteen or twenty years before the change in the millennium, as we shall shortly see. As a result, now one must instead regard each of the four quadrants as being composed not only of traditional denominations but also and more particularly of Christians whose greatest, but not total, set of persuasions is toward the form of Christian practice named in a particular box. For that reason, the original shape of the quadrilateral has been changed of late to resemble something nearer to a cruciform presentation like this:

The Cruciform

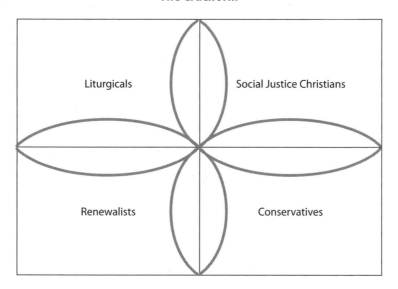

There is an old joke which contends that it makes a difference which sy-LAB-ble one puts the em-PHAS-is on. That is true in this case as well. That is, both Roman Catholicism as a branch of the faith and Roman Catholics as practitioners of the faith are famous for their deep concern for, and involvement in, issues of social justice. It would therefore be hugely inaccurate to think that they, as Liturgicals, have no interest or stake in Social Justice. By the same token, Methodists who, by tradition as well as founding, sit squarely in the Social Justice box, are equally famous for their development of new Christian liturgies, not to mention their adaptations of traditional ones.

What the boxes mean, in other words, is that one locates oneself or one's faith community on the map in terms of that which is more, or most, important in one's Christian practice. The two intersecting axes, consequently, should be visualized not as arbitrary or hard-and-fast lines meant to contain but rather as convenient and pliant demarcations intended only to clarify. In either case, the tension between the two upper boxes is still St. Paul's very ancient one of that between faith and works. That is, if on a Sabbath morning at 11:00 a.m.—and only at 11:00 a.m.—one can either build a habitat for humanity or go to the mass, the Social Justice Christian will say that faith without works is meaningless and go build the house, albeit with some regret. The Liturgical will counter that works without faith are empty and go to participate in the mass, likewise with some regret. Each constituency, in other words, will almost always have some exercise in the other's quadrant of concern.

Even as Liturgicals can be very concerned with social justice, though, so too can they be very definitely charismatic and/or Pentecostal. Or conversely, more and more often nowadays, fully charismatic congregations are incorporating forms of ancient liturgy in their worship, while at the same time exploring very conservative theology and exegesis. And so it goes—semi-permeable lines of division that mean to suggest places on a spectrum rather than absolute boundaries.

Just as there is a reason for the vertical axis of the original quadrilateral, so too there is a distinction being made by the horizontal one. That is, those Christians and communions above the center axis are placed there and together because, in general, for both of those quadrants what one *does* religiously is more central to his or her understanding of Christian living than is what one *believes* doctrinally. Conversely, the Christians and communions below the horizontal axis are placed there together because for them what one doctrinally *believes* is more central than what one *does* religiously. Nowhere in this should anybody assume that religiously or ritually based actions don't matter to Southern Baptists or that beliefs and creeds don't matter to Presbyterians. That is simply (and dangerously) not true. The distinction, rather, is in the definition, site, and centrality of the rectitude exercised by each.

Thus, one can be a very devout Episcopalian and be a bit conflicted—openly so even—about the historicity of the Virgin Birth. But what one would never do is allow a bit of wine spilt from the chalice to remain on the floor for the altar guild to wipe up with a rag later. Rather, one must immediately (or as soon as one notices the drop) stoop down and either use the purificator or take upon one's finger or fingers the blood of Our Lord and consume it there and then, grit and all. Or, should one be a mainline or Social Justice Lutheran and be in charge of making the new "fair linen" for the dressing of the communion table, one must be sure to put the precise and required number of stitches in each inch of those linens. Otherwise, the work will have to be ripped out and redone, because there is holy significance and symbolic importance to each of the numbers of stitches assigned to each piece of the work. Such emphasis on religious action or physicality is called *orthopraxy*, an adaptation from Greek for the concept of "right" or "correct" (*ortho*) practice (*praxis*).

By contrast, a devout Southern Baptist traditionally believes homosexuality is moral sin and a religious offense, yet he or she may have gay friends and beloved homosexual relatives. Keeping company with such friends and relatives is perfectly all right, so long as one remains clear that they are sinners. The old cliché of "hate the sin, love the sinner" is usually the rhetoric of choice for negotiating the resulting conundrum. In the same way, drinking is wrong, but an occasional drink with Roman Catholic friends for the sake of neighborliness, for instance, is acceptable so long as one perceives real drinking as religious transgression or infraction. Such emphasis on intellectual allegiance to doctrinal and moral codes is known as *orthodoxy*, again from the Greek and meaning "right" or "correct" doctrine or belief.

The Gathering Center

But these distinctions, too, are semi-permeable and allow the bowing of the horizontal lines, the result being a rounder, more cordial, or cruciform, presentation of the four major divisions in historic North American Christianity as it came into the closing decades of the twentieth century. What happened during those decades in the sociopolitical, economic, cultural, and intellectual context of the Great Emergence was to have the greatest imaginable impact on the cruciform diagram, however, and change it to something like this:

The Gathering Center

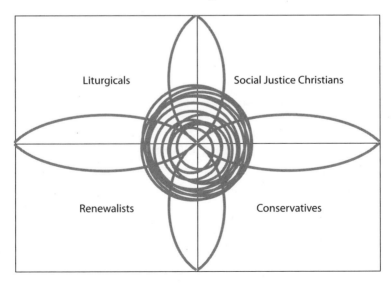

The twentieth century in the United States was characterized by many things, none of them more obvious than our originally slow, and eventually rapid, shift from being a rural to being an urban people. As the decades rolled along, more and more of us left the open spaces of pastures and plains for the defined ones of streets and neighborhoods. We laid aside as well the isolation and occasional socializing of country living for the constant companionship and unavoidable socializing of town and city life. Before the century's end, millions of us would not even be living in suburban neighborhoods any longer, but rather in the much tighter confines of apartment houses or condo complexes or multifamily buildings. Likewise, instead of earning our livelihood in solitary or near-solitary labor, more and more of us were earning it in offices or factories or commercial enterprises where we were in constant and fairly intimate contact with one another for the bulk of every working day.

Religion is very important to Americans and always has been. Statistically, it preoccupies or to some extent informs almost 90 percent of us; and nobody can even begin to gauge how much of our conversation is shaped around, or concerned with, it. The inevitable result, then, of our predisposition toward religious discussion and the increasing intensity of our contact with one another in both our private and working lives, was a construct that religion observers were, by the 1980s, beginning to refer to as *watercooler theology*.

Where once the country parson or the Holy Bible and family tradition about what it said had been the fount from which theology flowed, if it flowed at all, now popular opinion began to carry the day. Or if it did not carry the day, it certainly stirred up the questions. How could it fail to? For not only was there conversation about God-matters, but there was also a sudden diversity in the conversationalists gathered in the break room or chatting in the halls or swapping opinions on the elevator about the proper interpretation of current events.

Now the good Roman Catholic had to hear—or at least listen to—the spin an evangelical put on euthanasia; and the dyed-in-the-wool Presbyterian had to consider tales of miraculous healing from Church of God in Christ folk who had seen the thing itself actually happen. Evangelicals, by default and unintentionally, began to hear things about, and observe lives governed by, liturgical seasons and unfathomable popish practices like observing fixed-hour prayer. Staid American Baptists heard about Taizé and found themselves buying into the whole thing, but so too did their Southern Baptist cousins to whom they hadn't spoken in over a century. And so it went. The center was beginning to form. The old, natal divisions were beginning to melt away, especially there where their four corners met.

It was a slow process at first; and it certainly was an unintentional and unselfconscious one. It was just people—people swapping stories and habits, people admiring the ways of some other people whom they liked, people curious and able now to ask without offense. And more than anything else, it was people finding deep within themselves an empty spot or some niggling hunger or a restive, questioning impatience they had not experienced before, or at least had not been empowered to acknowledge before. So the swapping back and forth in public conversation and socializing went on.

As changes go, this one was aggravated or expedited, depending on one's point of view, by the fact that we were for the first time in history living not only in constant physical proximity with one another but also in subjective proximity. We were living in a media age. Newspapers, magazines, radio, television, and in one mighty burst of glory, the Internet saw to it that ideas flew about like bees in an overturned hive. We not only knew what everybody else was thinking, but we were able to counter and then be countered, back and forth unendingly, about ideas and values and meaningfulness—ideas and values that, ultimately, were about God and life and how it is to be lived. Religion, in other words. And watercooler theology, by the 1990s, had given way to ubiquitous theology, public, shared, and incredibly vital, even by this country's standards.

American religion had never had a center before, primarily because it was basically Protestant in its Christianity; and Protestantism, with its hallmark characteristic of divisiveness, has never had a center. Now one was emerging, but what was emerging was no longer Protestant.[3] It was no longer any "thing," actually. It was simply itself, a mélange of "things" cherry-picked from each quadrant and put together—some would say cobbled together—without any original intention and certainly with no design beyond that of conversation.

Since established churches, regardless of the quadrant in which they were located, could not accommodate such an ill-defined and amorphous presentation of the faith, the new faithful began to meet among themselves and hold worship services among and with those of like spirit. The house church movement began and then quietly boomed, as did such outré things as pub theology and bowling alley masses. In time, of course, some of these gatherings would grow into nondenominational churches. Some have become domestic communities and are eventuating in what we now call "the new monasticism," a way of being in which Christians, bound together under vows of stability, live out their private lives together in radical obedience to the Great Commandment. Other gatherings of emergents have no site at all and roam from public park to football stadium to Seventh-day Adventist churches to high school gyms, as the case may be in any given week. Some others, from time to time, fall heir, for a song, to old and abandoned church buildings which they occupy but feel only slight need to "fix up" in the traditional sense. All, however, share one shining characteristic: they are incarnational. Not only is Jesus of Nazareth incarnate God, but Christian worship must be incarnate as well. It must involve the body in all its senses and take place among people, all of whom are embraced equally and as children of God.

There is enormous energy in centripetal force, especially as it gathers more and more of its own kind into itself. Centripetal force, though, is usually envisioned by us as running downward, like the water in a bathtub drain. The gathering force of the new Christianity did the opposite. It ran upward and poured itself out, like some bursting geyser, in expanding waves of influence and nourishment. Where once the corners had met, now there was a swirling center, its centripetal force racing from quadrant to quadrant in ever-widening circles, picking up ideas and people from each, sweeping them into the center, mixing them there, and then spewing them forth into a new way of being Christian, into a new way of being Church.

The whole progression from distinct corners to a gathering center was precisely and exactly what sociologists and observers of religion had predicted would happen. The fact that the emerging pattern was following a predictable trajectory did not at first seem to inform most established churches and their governing bodies, however. What they saw, by and large and only at first, was a generational issue: the young were leaving as the young always do, as the boomers had done and the Gen-Xers after them. This was just some of those recalcitrant Gen-Xers mixed with the Millennials and not really doing anything much more significant than kicking up their theological heels a bit. They would come to their senses and come home to Mother Church under whatever defining adjectives or surnames she might live.

The error in this assessment—and as an assessment it did not last long—is that it failed to take into account the rummage sale factor. It failed to understand that we had slipped our moorings, at least temporarily. As a whole culture, as a social unit, we had at last become truly post-modern, post-denominational, post-rational, post-Enlightenment, post-literate, post-almost everything else that only a century before we had been, including post-Christendom. And these emergents, whose numbers increasingly included the white-haired as well as the young, could now use the term *inherited church* to name the goods being placed on the rummage sale table. Inherited church was that from which they had come and to which they, literally, now had no means of returning, let alone any desire at all to do so.

Backlash

Whenever there is so cataclysmic a break as is the rupture between modernity and postmodernity or, to put it in religious terms, between inherited church and emergent church, there is inevitably a backlash. Dramatic change is perceived as a threat to the status quo, primarily because it is. There must be a reaction in response. The codification of fundamentalism in the early twentieth century was arguably the earliest of the clearly demarcated reactions to the cultural and social changes out of which the Great Emergence is rising. There have been innumerable others since, and there undoubtedly are untold numbers still to come before all is said and done. But reaction is not in and of itself a destructive or even a malignant thing.

As scholars and commentators began to build and then adapt the quadrant way of describing and predicting a course for North American Christianity, they postulated that somewhere between 9 and 13 percent of those Christians natal to each quadrant would push back violently against the gathering force or pull of the center. At that point, the diagram came to look like this:

The Rose

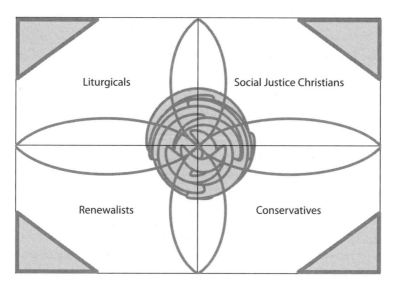

What commentators predicted, in other words, was that within each quadrant there would be congregations or ecclesial units and/or individuals who would aggressively dedicate themselves and their resources to reversing all the changes that had enabled, and were continuing to enable, the center and the emergence taking place there. Perhaps the most vivid example of this process, and certainly the one most often covered by the media, has occurred within the Episcopal Church in the United States where the ordination of an openly homosexual bishop forced the issue of *sola scriptura, scriptura sola* into the position of becoming a clear line in the sand. Choosing sides was unavoidable.[4]

This same process is, of course, occurring in all four quadrants, though just not quite as publicly. In the Social Justice quadrant, for example, the Presbyterian Church in the United States of America (but note well, not Presbyterianism per se) is suffering great losses as North American Presbyterianism splinters into various pieces. Entities like the American Presbyterian Church, the Orthodox Presbyterians, the Bible Presbyterians, the Evangelical Presbyterians, the Presbyterian Church in America, etc., etc. are shirring away as faithful, Reformation Christians struggle to find their balance again by dropping back to ideas and tenets that were their birthright. And thus it goes, each quadrant developing, in its upper and outer corner, a numerically minor, but psychologically significant configuration of reactionists or purists, again depending on who is doing the naming.

The quadrilateral that grew to cruciform shape with a centripetal center now takes on a different presentation. It looks more like the sketch of a stylized and perfectly centered flower, set off by a surround of petals and leaves. That is not a bad image. In fact, it is so compelling that what once was a quadrilateral sometimes is referred to now as a rose instead, or as *the* rose; and increasingly as "the new rose." The rose itself was the chosen symbol of the Great Reformation, the means by which early protesters could safely signal their allegiances. There is, therefore, a kind of sweet continuity in having a new rose for a new time. That image, however sweet, is not perhaps as apt as one might wish in one respect, though. In point of fact, the more realistic imaging of what the reacting outer corners have added is verbal and nautical rather than visual and aesthetic. That is, one is better served by thinking once more of that cable of meaning and of the small boat it connects to the immense dock.

No ship, even a tethered one, can stay safely afloat and in place unless it has some ballast to hold its courses against those of the rocky sea it sits in. Thus, while ballast is neither an attractive word or an appealing concept, it enjoys the countering advantages of inestimable importance and absolute usefulness. In the Great Emergence, reacting Christians are the ballast. However unattractive they may seem to be to other of their fellow Christians and however unattractive nonreacting Christians may seem to be to them, the small, outer percentage is the Great Emergence's ballast; and its function is as necessary and central to the success of this upheaval as is any other part of it. If the boat is not to tip and swamp, the ballast that forestalls too hasty a set of movements in a stormy sea must be there. One of the great dangers of what North America is going through is that some of her Christians, of whatever stripe, may cease to honor and accept the necessary function of all her Christians.

The Surrounding Currents

If observers can assign a rough percentage to the outer corners of each quadrant, can they do something similar with the rest of the rose? The answer is yes, more or less; but doing so will destroy the visual image of a flower.

How many emergent and emerging Christians are there right now in North America? Who knows? The truth, in fact, is that nobody is exactly sure who should and should not be labeled as an "emergent" or "emerging." There is, instead, a spectrum or kind of sliding scale out from the center of the quadrilateral into a widening ring of circles. To set those circles in place on the map, we have to return to the quadrilateral and re-sketch it as in the following illustration.

While no observer is willing to say emphatically just how many North American Christians are definitively emergent at the moment, it is not unreasonable to assume that by the time the Great Emergence has reached maturity, about 60 percent of practicing American Christians will be emergent or some clear variant thereof. If that be a fair estimate, then there should be a remaining 30 or 35 percent of American Christians, give or take a few points, who are neither reacters nor emergers. What can one know about them? A good deal, actually.

The Surrounding Currents

This illustration is not drawn to scale; in actuality, the outer circles constitute only about a third of what North American Christianity may look like in the near future.

It would seem that what is happening presently is a kind of sorting out of that neither-fish-nor-fowl 30 or more percent into four definable groups that, like everything else in the Great Emergence, have fairly soft or interpenetrating boundary lines between them. The outermost channel or current—that which is farthest from the center and nearest to the reactionary, outer corners—is peopled by persuaded quadrant dwellers. Like those who have fallen heir to Grandpa's old home place and who still like things just the way he had them, they see no need either to fight with the neighbors or to change the furniture. They will be Christian in an inherited church and know themselves to be both well served and good keepers of the family faith.

Like the reactionaries, these traditionalists lend stability to a faith in transition. Unlike the reactionaries, however, they will accommodate to, and serve as agents of, gradual change. Some of them will acquiesce to—maybe even assist in—the reconfiguration in their particular quadrants; and others, eventually, will participate in the realignments across sectarian lines that will become the adjusted Protestantism and amended Roman Catholicism of a "Counter-Emergence."

What Butler Bass describes so aptly and well as "re-traditioning" Christians are, as a group, those just one ring nearer to the center. The re-traditionalists have also chosen to stay with their inherited church, but at the same time they energetically wish to make it more fully what it originally was. Like fond refurbishers who have inherited a much-loved and historic house, they seek to update the wiring, install better plumbing, and modernize the kitchen, but not in order to sell the house. Quite the contrary. They want to live in it for all of time, while simultaneously increasing its comfortableness, enhancing its natural beauty, and exposing its welcoming worth to all who pass by. In many ways, theirs is the most remarkable, arduous, and ultimately richest task of all.

Very close to the re-traditioners and, at times, almost indistinguishable from them are the Progressive Christians. One track nearer to the center, they feel its pull more; and while wanting to maintain their position in institutional Christianity, they want also to wrestle with what they see as the foolheartedness of holding on to dogma-based ideas and doctrinally restricted governance and praxis. Even while remaining well within their Reformation-based communions, they seek to adapt what they have to the realities of postmodernity.

They also are like householders who have inherited a house; but instead of being refurbishers, they are remodelers. For them, it makes more sense not to restore what one has by retouching its former beauty, but rather to simply open the whole place up a bit more. Progressives, accordingly, can with confidence remove some inconvenient walls, replace some drafty windows, and even knock off an obstructing porch or two without sensing any damage to the integrity of the family home. Thus, Eric Elnes, one of Progressive Christianity's most dynamic and influential young leaders, once, half in jest, defined a Progressive as being "anyone who believes in loving God, neighbor, and self, and thinks that two out of three ain't bad."[5]

Nearest to the emergent center, but still distinct from it, are the "hyphenateds," their name being a bit tongue-in-cheek, of course. Tongue-in-cheek or not, though, they all do indeed bear either literal or implied hyphens as part of the names by which they call themselves. They are the Presby-mergents, the Metho-mergents, the Angli-mergents, the Luther-mergents, and so on. And in their hyphening of their self-assumed names, they recognize that theirs is probably the most schizophrenic of the encompassing circles. In some ways, however, it is also the most vibrant and colorful, exceeding at times even the vitality and rigor of the center itself.

Life on the margins has always been the most difficult and, at the same time, the one most imaginatively lived. Certainly that seems to be the situation with the hyphenateds, making it difficult to predict exactly where they will finally land. Will they remain within their quadrants and, like the traditionalists, re-traditioners, and progressives, become an informing part of what their respective quadrants or newly allied communions reconfigure into being? Or will they be drawn ever more forcefully into the swirling center, in the end leaving their natal communities entirely behind? Probably there will be no uniformity of resolution. Some will drop back, some will move to the center, some perhaps will stay as they are. Time will tell. But for the moment, the hyphenateds are also householders who, having fallen heir to Grandpa's old home place, feel a compelling need to honor the land it sits upon and the trees that surround it, but no need to retain its structural shape. Imaginatively enough, though, while they may tear down the house, they will salvage some of the material out of which it was built and incorporate those honored bricks and columns, plinths and antique doors into the new thing they are building.

And that brings the discussion back to the center again, to that emerging, a-borning center which will be the next to hold pride of place in Christian history. Can we look from here and make out enough of the contours of that forming, but still amorphous, mass to predict what it is going to look like over the next two or three decades? Given what we know of it and what we know from historical patterns, can we extrapolate from there some useful sense of direction about where we are going? Yes . . . or at least to some extent . . . we can.

---

1. Paul Raushenbusch, ed., *Christianity and the Social Crisis in the 21st Century: The Classic That Woke Up the Church* (New York: HarperOne, 2007), 40. Walter Rauschenbusch's great classic, *Christianity and the Social Crisis,* was re-released in 2007 in a centennial edition edited by his great-grandson, Paul Raushenbush, and with accompanying essays and commentary by eight contemporary scholars.

2. Every honest writer, especially one with any academic experience at all, knows the tension inherent in talking about work that has no one, single, footnotable originator to whom credit can be given. Yet, and at the same time, when the writer has himself or herself been one of the commentators who has refined, amended, and updated an evolving concept, one can hardly disavow the result. Accordingly, what is right and correct here and in the rest of this volume is hardly of my own creation, though much of its adaptation is. What proves to have been in error, I will take responsibility for.

3. The earliest presentations of the shift away from Protestantism as it is traditionally defined presented as "independent" churches or as

"community" churches or as "interdenominational" churches. By whatever name one chooses to call them, they all, by and large, were and still are hybrids. In matters so fundamental as their very composition, they eschew Protestantism, their theater seats being filled at every service by believers from every part of the Christian spectrum—Roman Catholic to Assemblies of God and back again. In point of fact, the membership of a community church today often draws about a quarter of its members from each of the quadrants.

Because, however, the initial energy of the gathering center was evangelical in origin, these early independent or interdenominational churches—for example, Lakewood Church in Houston (founded 1959) or Willow Creek just outside Chicago in South Barrington (founded 1975)—were more evangelical than emergent. Their evangelicalism did indeed jump the old barriers of sectarian creeds, but it retained the fervor of midcentury Protestantism's belief in an all-encompassing, all-providing institution. It retained as well the central core of evangelism, *sola scriptura, scriptura sola.*

In times of enormous and apparently chaotic change, the security of a drop-back position is almost irresistible; and *sola scriptura* was the ultimate in drop-back positions or even is just plain, simple retreat from indecipherable chatter. The megachurch phenomenon is the result and can legitimately be parsed as evangelicalism's first institutionalized response to the force of the Great Emergence.

4. It would appear that the predictions of 9 to 13 percent in reactionary movement is a bit high, at least in this case. Current estimates of the percentage of Episcopalian parishes, bishops, and dioceses that will eventually break away from the national church and align themselves with more traditional forms of Anglicanism is going to come in at around 7 percent. What cannot yet be predicted is the global implications and repercussions of all this, for international considerations lie outside the purview of this discussion and schematic.

5. In a personal conversation with the author in 2007 and used with permission. Elnes's *The Phoenix Affirmations* (Jossey-Bass, 2006) stands today as the clearest, most articulate presentation of Progressive Christianity.

7

The Way Ahead

Mapping Fault Lines and Fusions

In speaking earlier of the axes of the original quadrilateral, we noted that the horizontal one suggests a separation of sorts between the amount of emphasis placed by those in each quadrant on correct action—orthopraxy—and/or that placed on correct belief—orthodoxy. In the course of that discussion, we made mention in passing of the vertical axis and of what was its defining purpose. We need now to look a bit more closely at that vertical; for much of the genius of the quadrilateral is the carefulness with which each part was originally placed within the whole.

Different Bases of Authority

The question of "Where now is our authority?" is, as we have noted, always the central and overarching one in every time of upheaval. The Great Emergence will be no different from its predecessors in this regard. Basically, however, North American Christianity entered into the time of emergence already possessed of some relative difference of opinion about where authority lies. That is, those Christians in the quadrants to the left of the vertical axis have always acknowledged a base of authority that is slightly or vastly different, depending upon one's point of view, from the authority base asserted by those in the quadrants to the right of the axis. Those to the right are quite clear that *sola scriptura, scriptura sola* is indeed the foundational source from which all authority flows. Those to the left of the vertical axis are not so sure, however. In fact, historically, they have never been willing to take quite such an unmediated position.

While also honoring Scripture, those on the left have argued that holy writ is only one among several sources of authority open to Christians. For the Renewalists, there is no question but that the Holy Spirit is an active, effectuating agent in every part of time and space. What, therefore, the Spirit teaches a believer in revelation and infusion must be honored as a principal form or source of direction. To not admit of this ongoing process is, for the Renewalists, arrogantly to confine God Himself to the pages of a very old book.

Liturgicals, in the upper left, are likewise in agreement that confining God to a fixed set of words is infamy. They are a bit more chary, however, of direct inspiration that has not been tested by the ages and by common sense or filtered through the apostolic thinking of those called and ordained and trained for such discerning. But then, they are even more fearful of any employments of the Bible that have not also been so filtered. One of the most informing tensions in the Great Emergence, as it struggles to resolve the authority question, lies just here, along the vertical axis of the quadrilateral; but things have changed a bit more than that since the original quadrilateral was drawn up.

Where once we had four quadrants with a vertical axis and only one horizontal one, we actually no longer have a quadrilateral at all.

The diagram must now be adjusted to reflect the changes caused by the active presence of the emerging center. That is, the earlier horizontal axis must be split into two lines, the one well below and the other well above the old center axis. When one does that, the original diagram changes to look like this:

The Bases of Authority (a)

	Liturgicals		Social Justice Christians
Orthopraxy			
Orthodoxy	Renewalists		Conservatives

Orthonomy and Theonomy

Orthopraxy (right practice) still remains in place as the defining characteristic of those Christians choosing to remain solidly in place somewhere in the upper quadrants; and orthodoxy (right doctrine) does the same for those still resident somewhere in the lower quadrants. In both cases, however, their numbers are greatly diminished. The center, on the other hand—the emergence itself—is growing in numbers and by definition occupies no quadrant, coming instead from all of them. Where, then, is authority for the Great Emergence and for the form of Christianity it is fashioning for the centuries ahead?

On both the left and the right sides of the vertical axis, the space abutting that emerging center is blank. It may remain so, in fact, for many years. For so long as it does, however, the debate among the contending candidates for the right of final authority will be a major as well as a bitter one. It is nonetheless possible to sketch in with broad strokes where the argument is and something of the battleground on which it will be fought. To do that, we must adjust, for one last time, the quadrilateral by adding two words—or near neologisms, if one prefers—to each of those blank side spaces.

The Bases of Authority (b)

"Ortho" is still the anglicized form of the Greek for "correct" or right. The suffix "-nomy" is a relatively new youngster on the block, however. Or perhaps it is not so much new, as new in this context, *orthonomy* itself having been borrowed from philosophy where it has a somewhat different connotation. Either way, "-nomy" is also an anglicization and derives from *nomos*, a Greek word that is almost impossible to define adequately in English. Pythagorean originally in use and almost mystical in connotation, it means to name the principles or resonances that create the harmony of sounds in poetry or music and the order in things in creation. It is also the word used in the Septuagint and in the Christian New Testament to name the Law and its perfection as the expression of the governance of God. In sum, *nomos* is, most nearly, the ineffable beauty in that which is divine, especially as it becomes incarnate within space and time.

Orthonomy may be defined then as a kind of "correct harmoniousness" or beauty. In effect, when it is used as here, it means the employment of aesthetic or harmonic purity as a tool for discerning the truth—and therefore the intent and authority—of anything, be that thing either doctrine or practice. Thus it is very common to find that many emergent Christians are genuinely confused and befuddled by Reformation Protestants' constant wrestling with modernist questions of historicity. An emergent, in observing heated debates or impassioned conversations about the factualness of the Virgin birth, for example, can truly be puzzled. For him or her, the whole "problem" is just not "there" in any distinguishable or real sense. For the emergent, as he or she will be quick to say, the Virgin birth is so beautiful that it has to be true, whether it happened or not.

At first blush, this is such a refreshing approach and such a relief from droning theological arguments that one wants to embrace it immediately. A good rabbi—Judaism has wrestled with the matter long enough to know it well—will be quick to point out, however, that what one has in orthonomy, when used thus, is no more than a new rendition of an old error. To be exact, it is a variation upon what is known as "the Keatsian heresy," after John Keats and his famous observation that truth is beauty, and beauty is truth. Beauty, in point of fact, rests in the eye of the beholder, to quote another famous cliché. It is, therefore, subject to all the conditioning and interpretive filtering of human culture. An action or object is not, in other words, divine or holy or authoritative simply by virtue of appearing beautiful or harmonious or even efficacious.

To counter the tendency toward allowing aesthetic response and/or emotionally or spiritually moving experience to become bases for authority, emergents and emergings on the right of the vertical have reactivated or reconfigured a word of their own: *theonomy.*[1] Obvious in its derivation from the Greek *theos* (god) as well as from *nomos*, this combination is in far wider circulation than is its counterpart, having been actively present in the discussion since midcentury. As a term, it means to say or name the principle that only God can be the source of perfection in action and thought. The question, of course, is how best to pierce through to His meaning, the Bible itself being the only "source" of authority as well as the one readiest to hand for those who hold with theonomy.

As is patently clear, the burden of the argument of theonomy is still the principle of *sola scriptura*, albeit in more modish and culturally attractive clothes, while orthonomy is only a variant of tradition, reason, and inspiration as conduits for safely receiving the holy. Neither is sufficient by itself, yet they seem antithetical, one to the other. Then again, maybe not.

Networked Authority

The new Christianity of the Great Emergence must discover some authority base or delivery system and/or governing agency of its own. It must formulate—and soon—something other than Luther's

sola scriptura which, although used so well by the Great Reformation originally, is now seen as hopelessly outmoded or insufficient,
even after it is, as here, spruced up and re-couched in more current
sensibilities.

Over the course of previous hinge times, the Church has always
been sucked along in the same ideational currents as has the culture
in general, especially in matters of governance. The result has been
that, at any given time, the political structure of one has always
been reflected in and/or exercised influence upon the organiza-
tional structures of the other. Gregory the Great, in wrapping up
the chaos of the sixth century, created a Church run by monasteries and convents, a system that was in every way analogous to the
manors and small fiefdoms of Europe's Dark Ages. The Roman
Church, in emerging from the Great Schism, positioned the exercise and definition of authority in a single position, the Papacy,
and the council of appointed cardinals surrounding that throne.
As a pattern, it was a religious expression of the system of kings
and lords growing up in the centuries of pre-Reformation culture.
The Reformation, with its shift to the democratic theology of the
priesthood of all believers and its insistence on literacy for the sake
of *sola scriptura*, created a governance exercised by elected leaders subject, in theory anyway, to the will of the people whom they
served. Modern Protestant bodies reflect this flow of authority for
the same reason that America herself does. Both are products of
the same stimuli and circumstances. Given all of that, what logi-
cally can be expected of the Great Emergence, especially in terms
of authority in religion?

When one asks an emergent Christian where ultimate authority
lies, he or she will sometimes choose to say either "in Scripture" or
"in the Community." More often though, he or she will run the two
together and respond, "in Scripture and the community." At first

blush, this may seem like no more than a thoughtless or futile effort to make two old opposites cohabit in one new theology; but that does not appear to be what is happening here. What is happening is something much closer to what mathematicians and physicists call *network theory.*

That is, a vital whole—in this case, the Church, capital C—is not really a "thing" or entity so much as it is a network in exactly the same way that the Internet or the World Wide Web or, for that matter, gene regulatory and metabolic networks are not "things" or entities. Like them and from the point of view of an emergent, the Church is a self-organizing system of relations, symmetrical or otherwise, between innumerable member-parts that themselves form subsets of relations within their smaller networks, etc., etc. in interlacing levels of complexity.

The end result of this understanding of dynamic structure is the realization that no one of the member parts or connecting networks has the whole or entire "truth" of anything, either as such and/or when independent of the others. Each is only a single working piece of what is evolving and is sustainable so long as the interconnectivity of the whole remains intact. No one of the member parts or their hubs, in other words, has the whole truth as a possession or as its domain. This conceptualization is not just theory. Rather, it has a name: *crowd sourcing;* and crowd sourcing differs from democracy far more substantially than one might at first suspect. It differs in that it employs total egalitarianism, a respect for worth of the hoi polloi that even pure democracy never had, and a complete indifference to capitalism as a virtue or to individualism as a godly circumstance.[2]

The duty, the challenge, the joy and excitement of the Church and for the Christians who compose her, then, is in discovering what it means to believe that the kingdom of God is within one and in understanding that one is thereby a pulsating, vibrating bit in a much grander network. Neither established human authority nor scholarly or priestly discernment alone can lead, because, being human, both are trapped in space/time and thereby prevented from a perspective of total understanding. Rather, it is how the message runs back and forth, over and about, the hubs of the network that it is tried and amended and tempered into wisdom and right action for effecting the Father's will.

Thus, when pinned down and forced to answer the question, "What is Emergent or Emerging Church?" most who are will answer, "A conversation," which is not only true but which will always be true. The Great Emergence can not "be," and be otherwise. Furthermore, whatever else such a conceptualizing may be, it is certainly and most notably global, recognizing none of the old, former barriers of nationality, race, social class, or economic status. It is also radical . . . and it is predictably our future both in this model as the relational, nonhierarchal, a-democratized form of Christianity entering into its hegemony and as an analog for the political and social principles of authority and organization that will increasingly govern global life during the centuries of the Great Emergence.

The Great Emergence's movement toward a system of ecclesial authority that waits upon the Spirit and rests in the interlacing lives of Bible-listening, Bible-honoring believers undoubtedly has some of its impetus in the sensibilities of the secular Great Emergence around it. It nonetheless has found most of its power tools and construction theory not in the culture per se but in the theology and experience of the quadrants and, significantly, in one non-quadrant group.

A Gift from the Quakers

The Great Emergence as a religious reconfiguration in Christianity had its earliest proponents and energy in evangelicalism. In fact, there was once a time when many scholars argued (and a few still do) that the Great Emergence was simply crypto-Evangelicalism and would go away in time, swamped by its own gravitas. That has not happened; but neither does its failure to happen unsay the fact that the first, early signs of restiveness and change happened in the lower, right-hand quadrant of the original quadrilateral and swirled from there leftward, up, and around.

The Conservative quadrant, however, did not have native to it any unifying or cohering way of maintaining biblical authority in a postmodern, post-rational, post-Enlightenment time. It lacked the flexibility in both imagination and practice required to shift from democratic systems of organization to those of network theory, affinity grouping, and open source discernment. Yet wedged between that lower, right-hand quadrant of the Conservatives and the quadrant just above them of Social Justice Christians was a discrete body of Christians who did.

Both by heritage and by virtue of having always been middlers belonging in nobody's camp, the Quakers have from the beginning had a distinctly "other" easiness with the paradoxical interplay of revelation, discernment, and Scripture in the life and governance of the body of Christ on earth. Not exactly a refusal to engage questions of authority, Quaker thought chooses rather to assume that quiet engagement with God and the faithful reveals authority from the center out to other centers of engagement. Network theory, in other words, or at the very least, proto-network theory.

As a result, over the closing decades of the twentieth century, Quaker writers and theologians like Richard Foster and Parker Palmer and J. Brent Bill became more and more central to the life and thought of Christians gravitating toward the center. These Quaker writers instructed spiritually, certainly; but they also described, almost by default but still with great credibility, a different set of foundational approaches to orderly being. Almost as significantly, they became comforters and pastors to thousands of early emergence Christians who had forfeited both of these benisons by the simple process of moving toward the center. The most significant of them all, however, may turn out to have been John Wimber, one of the founders and arguably the leading theorist of the Association of Vineyard Churches and himself a Quaker.

During the last decade of the twentieth century, Donald E. Miller, Firestone Professor of Religion at the University of Southern California, came to be one of the most prominent and influential authorities on, and analysts of, the emergence phenomenon. He wrote:

> I believe that we are witnessing a new reformation that is transforming the way Christianity will be experienced in the new millennium. This reformation, unlike the one led by Martin Luther, is challenging not doctrine, but the medium through which the message of Christianity is articulated . . . these "new paradigm" churches have discarded many of the attributes of established religion. Appropriating contemporary cultural forms, these churches are creating a new genre of worship music, restructuring the organizational character of institutional religion, and democratizing access to the sacred by radicalizing the Protestant principle of the priesthood of all believers.[3]

Miller's scholarly work was concerned more with the changes that emergence was causing in Protestantism per se than it was with the whole of North American Christianity in the time of emergence. As a result, Miller came to isolate and describe what he refers to as "new paradigm" churches, by which he meant emergent forms of Protestantism that differed markedly from any forms that had preceded them, but which could hardly be expected to be either "a" or "the" final expression of what the new or post-Emergence Protestantism would eventually be. In his study, Miller identified three such groupings—The Vineyard, Calvary Chapels, and Hope Chapels—as being "new paradigms."

While Hope Chapels have remained vital and active, it is the other two of Miller's new paradigms that are of the greater interest here. Calvary Chapel, which calls itself a Fellowship of Churches, was founded in 1965 in Costa Mesa, California, by Chuck Smith Sr. Over the almost half century since, it has grown into a large network of congregations, some of them approaching megachurch size. It has also become, for the sociologist of religion, an absorbing case study in the tensions of emergence.

In the late 1970s, Chuck Smith Sr.'s son, Chuck Jr., established a Calvary Chapel at Capo Beach. Capo Beach rather quickly grew into the substantial and vibrant church it presently is, with Chuck Jr. serving as its senior pastor until 2007. Over the years, however, Smith Jr. began to become more and more interested in, and attracted to, ancient and/or liturgical Christian practices, wishing to weave them—and exposure to them—into his congregation's worship and thought. The result was that Capo Beach began more to resemble an emergent church than a Calvary Chapel per se.

By 2006, the distinctions in those two ways of being had become antithetical to one another, and the Capo Beach congregation was asked to remove itself from the affiliation of Calvary Chapels. Smith Jr., presently on sabbatical for a time of study and discernment, describes himself as one who is "convinced that something other than Evangelicalism is on the horizon. . . . I'm not emergent, I'm something else and I don't think there is a name for it."[4] All of that is a way of saying, of course, that the new paradigms, as early expressions of emergence, are subject to the same decisions that the hyphenateds are going to have to make: Which are we, and where do we belong?

The Vineyard Association of Churches, while hardly free of tensions and while certainly not escaping the questions of self-definition, has followed a somewhat different course, in no small part because of Wimber and his Quaker ways of being. Wimber, an adult convert to Christianity, attended a Quaker meeting in Yorba Linda, California, for several years during the 1960s and early '70s, becoming in the process a powerful evangelist who led literally hundreds of people to conversion. By 1974, he had become founding director of the Department of Church Growth at Fuller Theological Seminary, a position he would hold for almost five years.

During the Fuller years, a house church began in Wimber's home. Affiliated originally with his Quaker meeting, the group in time became first charismatic, and then so charismatic as to cause rupture with the Quakerism from which it had sprung. The Wimber congregation, predictably enough and shortly thereafter, outgrew the Wimber house and briefly joined itself to a Calvary Chapel. The differences between the two groups, especially over the gifts of the Spirit, became too great, however; and the Wimberites left to join what was, at that time, a very small group of churches known as the Vineyard Christian Fellowships.

It was Wimber, the former Quaker, who would transform that tiny clutch of like-minded proto-emergents into the Association of Vineyard Churches that now constitutes one of the few—some would say the only—examples of more or less traditionally structured emergence Christianity.[5] It was Wimber also who would articulate and popularize some of the theological principles needed to accelerate the pace of the gathering center. He spoke over and over again of "church-planting as the best form of evangelism." And "authenticity," now the *sine qua non* of the Great Emergence and in essence its tribal war cry, was a Wimber war cry first.

In his theory of "The Third Wave of the Holy Spirit," so named by his Fuller colleague, C. Peter Wagner, Wimber also managed to modify classic Pentecostalism enough so that thousands of Evangelicals and Conservatives, who were fearful of an exclusive emphasis on speaking in tongues, could embrace the Renewalist part of the quadrant without fear. Wimber simply argued that speaking in tongues was only one among many gifts of the Spirit taught in the Scripture and that to reject those gifts because of the particularities of one gift was itself foolhardy.

Center Set and Bounded Set

More portentously, Wimber, having cut his teeth on Quakerism, taught and publicized something very close to network theory, though he did not have those words at the time. He spoke instead of "center-set movement," of a Christianity whose basic gatherings would be clear about their vision and be busy about the work of the kingdom while letting people sort themselves out by how close each wanted to get to the center. Such an approach was—and still is—clearly a leap of enormous faith. That is, it assumes that something other than "rules" is holding things together while, at the same time, also preventing the whole construct from skittering off into chaos. In the final analysis, in other words, it places authority in the existing center.

The whole question of rules is, of course, a subset of the authority question. That is, the very presence of rules assumes some authority effecting them and some consequence for violating them. In addition to defining how things must be conceptualized and/or executed, rules also result in what Wimber called "bounded-set" groups. That is, among their other functions, rules also define the boundaries that determine who is in and who is out of a bounded-set group, but never of a center-set one. By the change of the millennium, emergent Christianity in general had adopted a center-set approach, though its leaders no longer use that terminology very frequently. More commonly, one will hear emergence leaders speak about the difference between "believe-behave-belong" and "belong-behave-believe." And while such a string of words seems at first to be more clever than substantive, first impressions can often be wrong. They certainly are in this instance.

The first triad of "believe-behave-belong" fits the bounded-set approach of both traditional Roman Catholicism and historic Protestantism. It requires adherence to certain rules of doctrinal belief and human conduct as prerequisites to membership in their ranks. The second triad, which occurs in the center-set or emergence approach, reverses the process. In center-set Christianity, one simply belongs to a gathering of Christians by virtue of a shared humanity and an affinity with the individuals involved in whatever the group as a whole is doing. And belonging may be as far into Christianity or Christian experience as a belonger wants to go. Should he or she, however, become desirous of more, or be led to more, or be convicted by association that there is more, then he or she will begin to behave in an un-superimposed iteration of the conduct and mode of thinking that informs the group as a whole. As behavior begins to condition living, it also begins to shape belief until the two become one . . . the center-set approach, in other words. And the difference between the two is indeed substantial.

Narrative

The Great Emergence is characterized, certainly, by more than one principle that at first blush seems so subtle as to be, if not insubstantial, then at least nonsubstantial. Both in its secular and its religious forms, emergence thinking has a mysticism that is often seen by its critics as amounting to anti-intellectualism. Probably nothing could possibly be any further from the truth. But then, probably nothing could possibly be more totally postmodern, either.

Emergents, because they are postmodern, believe in paradox; or more correctly, they recognize the ubiquity of paradox and are not afraid of it. Instead, they see in its operative presence the tension where vitality lives. To make that point, an emergent will quite often offer the most simplistic of proof texts: X squared = 4, and that is a fact. Since it is a fact, what is the value of X? Quite clearly, X = 2 . . . except, of course, X also quite clearly equals -2. What is one to make of that contradiction, that impossibility, that paradox?

For starters, what we in the first world have made of it is the bulk of all the technology and gimmicks that render our lives so much more comfortable than otherwise they would have been. The point, in other words, is that logic is not worth nearly so much as the last five hundred years would have had us believe. It is, therefore, not to be trusted as an absolute, nor are its conclusions to be taken as truth just because they depend from logical thinking. Very often, in fact, logic's fallacies result from logic's lack of a sufficient height or distance in its perspective. That is, logic suffers from the fact that it is human, not divine, and suffers all the limitations of humanity, including being irrevocably contained in time and space.

By extension, meta-narrative is likewise to be distrusted, being as it is also a product of humanity's human thinking and explaining. Narrative, on the other hand, is the song of the vibrating network. It is the spider's web in its trembling, a single touch on one strand setting all the others to resonating. Narrative circumvents logic, speaking the truth of the people who have been and of whom we are. Narrative speaks to the heart in order that the heart, so tutored, may direct and inform the mind.

In effect, such a position is not only a relational conceptualization of reality, but it is also the foundation of a markedly different principle of human organization and of the understanding of "self." Where exactly it will go remains to be seen, but go it will. There is no doubt about that. One of the two or three secondary but primal obligations facing the Great Emergence, as we have said, is the formulation of a working answer to the question of what exactly a human being is, not only as a single creature, but also as a part of a genus in creation.

The Problem with Constantine

But also running like lietmotivs through emergence conversation are some other, very down-to-earth and harrying concerns about meta-narrative. Not the least of them, in terms of the coming conflict between traditional Christian and emergence theology, is a growing distrust for the precepts and teachings of the post-Constantinian Church. Arguably, one of the most potentially destructive things that can happen to a faith is for it to become the accepted and established religion of the political, cultural, and social unit in which its adherents live. Certainly, there is no question that Constantine's preempting of Christianity in the fourth century was the great pivot point by means of which Christianity became a dominant institution. It is also the point at which the so-called Hellenization of the faith began to accelerate, infiltrate, and eventually dominate Christian theology.[6]

Doctrine as a codified part of Christianity was born under Constantine and was, among other things, formalized for his convenience. More consequential even than doctrine per se was Christianity's shift, under Constantine's protective aegis, from Judaism's wholistic theology and wholistic conceptualization of human life and structure to the dualism of Greek philosophy and of Greco-Roman culture. The whole purpose of "salvation" began to shift from a means of effecting or living out God's will on earth to being a ticket for transplantation into a paradisial hereafter. Gnosticism flourished as never before. The body became evil and therefore suspect.

More to the point, the body became a thing separate from the soul, whose definition as a result grew more and more nebulous even as it became more and more privatized and individualized. Whether or not extant Roman and/or Protestant Christian thought can or will revisit their foundational assumptions about such matters remains to be seen. The significant thing here is that the Great Emergence is doing so; and the theology that comes from that work will be the theology, in part, of society's reconfigured understanding of the self, the soul, the humanness of being in *imago dei*. It will impact everything from medical policy to moral theory as well as evangelism and religious formation.

Future Possibilities

Some of the impact of de-Hellenization on religious formation is already discernible. The actual nature of the Atonement, for example, or the tenet of an angry God who must be appeased or the question of evil's origins are suddenly all up for reconsideration.[7] If in pursuing this line of exegesis, the Great Emergence really does what most of its observers think it will, it will rewrite Christian theology—and thereby North American culture—into something far more Jewish, more paradoxical, more narrative, and more mystical than anything the Church has had for the last seventeen or eighteen hundred years.[8]

Regardless of what its theology eventually matures into, however, there is no question that the Great Emergence is the configuration of Christianity which is in ascendency. It is just as certain that both the Roman and the Protestant communions in North America will have to readjust themselves to accommodate the stresses of such massive changes in the culture and in the Church.

The Vatican presumably will influence the former's adaptations. But, as Miller clearly understood, it is in Protestantism that the adaptations will be the most dramatic. Within the near future, post-Emergence Protestantism will almost have to assume (indeed, some would say it already has begun to effect) a collegial congress of all its member parts that functions democratically and is class- and merit-based in oversight and authority. The seeds of that accommodation are already deep within its history.

What is not nearly so easy to discern just yet is how the Great Emergence will interface with the results and consequences of such realignments; and more than any other of North America's Christians, it is emergents themselves who are going to have to reconsider Emergence Christianity. They must begin now to think with intention about what this new form of the faith is and is to become; because what once was an engaging but innocuous phenomenon no longer is. The cub has grown into the young lion; and now is the hour of his roaring.

---

1. Since about 2004, there has been a still-small, but perhaps growing divergence within the ranks of those who call themselves center-dwellers. For that reason, this overview has frequently used the somewhat awkward phrase, "emergent and emerging" Christians to indicate that the two are not quite the same thing and may not ever come to be of one mind just as was true, for example, with the Reforming, Confessing, and Professing strands of the Great Reformation.

The principal point of the differences between contemporary emergents and emergings is, as one might suspect, in the orthonomy/theonomy conflict. Emergents, associated with and led by Christians like Brian McLaren, Tony Jones, Doug Pagitt, etc., would put more emphasis on orthonomy than on theonomy, were they forced to choose between, rather than integrate, the two. Emerging Christians, whose most visible and influential leaders are Dan Kimball and Erwin McManus, tend toward the theonomy side of things, finding it increasingly difficult to occupy the same theological ground as do emergents.

2. To more fully appreciate the nuances and radical comprehensiveness of these distinctions, the reader may want to see Brian McLaren's *Everything Must Change* (Thomas Nelson, 2007) or visit McLaren's related website.

3. Miller, a voluminous writer, but a careful and consistent observer, made this point in essentially these same words many, many times. The form quoted here is taken from *Thunderstruck—A Truck Stop for the Soul*, a website exemplary of where emergence as a conversation has for years been taking place. Readers who prefer their sources to be more traditional ones may want to look at Miller's bibliography. He introduces his *Reinventing American Protestantism: Christianity in the New Millennium*, for instance, with the words, "A revolution is transforming American Protestantism . . ." (Berkeley: University of California Press, 1997), 1.

4. Email to author from Chuck Smith Jr., March 19, 2008.

5. While staunchly refusing to be a denomination or to take on the apparatus of traditionally institutionalized church, the Association does have "overseers" who exercise something very close to episcopal oversight. It maintains as well a central office of sorts and convenes its pastors from time to time for discernment, prayer, instruction, and, to some limited extent, matters of Association business; yet it is entrepreneurial in governance at the congregational level, is egalitarian to a fault, regards itself as non-creedal, and uses "tribal" as an adjective of choice for describing its singular form of group affinity and affections.

6. Doug Pagitt, founding pastor of Solomon's Porch in Minneapolis and one of emergent Christianity's most influential leaders and brilliant thinkers, makes a spirited and detailed presentation of this whole area of concern in his *A Christianity Worth Believing* (Jossey-Bass, 2008).

7. In the same way that Martin Luther became the symbolic leader and spokesman for the Great Reformation, so too has Brian McLaren become the symbolic leader and spokesman for the Great Emergence. His 2005 volume, *A Generous Orthodoxy* (Zondervan) is both an analog to Luther's ninety-five theses and also a clearly stated overview of many of the parts of post-Constantinian Christian theology that are now undergoing reconsideration.

8. If such should indeed happen, then there is no overstatement or inflation in saying that the Great Emergence is not only a semi-millennial upheaval, but also a bi-millennial phenomenon. As many readers may know, Medieval mystics like Joachim of Fiore would regard that development as nothing less than prophetic fulfillment, inasmuch as they believed history

to be divided into bi-millennial units. For them, from the beginning to the birth of Christ was the two thousand years of primary emphasis on God the Father. From the coming of Christ to 2000 was to be the two thousand years of primary emphasis on God the Son. From 2000 CE to 4000 CE would be the two thousand years of the primacy in worship and in human affairs of God the Spirit. To complete the biblical scheme of seven millennia, the era from 4000 to 5000 CE will be the consummate and glorious union of all three parts of the Godhead within space/time.

Index

abortion, 102–3
Absolute, 89
addiction, 92
Adler, Alfred, 70
affinity grouping, 154
African-American Christianity, 84
Alcoholics Anonymous, 91–92
Aldrin, Buzz, 82
angels, 65, 78
anti-intellectualism, 159
Apostolic Church, 27
aristocracy, 51
Aristotle, 30
Armstrong, Karen, 30–31
Armstrong, Neil, 82
artificial intelligence, 70, 71, 106
Asberry, Richard and Ruth, 83
Asian spirituality, 96
Assemblies of God, 127
Association of Vineyard Churches, 155,
    156–58, 164n5
atheism, 90
atonement, 162
Augustinian theology, 27
authenticity, 157
authority, 72–73, 145–50, 158
    of clergy, 92–93
    as experiential, 85

in Great Emergence, 85, 150–53
    and re-formation, 45
    of Scripture, 82, 151
automobile, 85–87, 90, 108, 114
"Axial Age," 30
Azusa Street Revival, 83–84, 91

Babylonian Captivity, 29
ballast, 138–39
Bass, Diana Butler, 28, 58, 141
beauty, 149–50
becoming, 88
beliefnet.com, 106
beliefs, 130
"believe-behave-belong," 159
"belong-behave-believe," 159
Benedict, St., 22
Benedict XIII, 44
Bhagavad-Gita, 30
biblical absolutism, 101
biblical criticism, 65
biblical literacy, 87, 102, 115–16
Big Bang, 82
Bill, J. Brent, 154
biology, 65
birth control pill, 113
birth rates, 115
Black Death, 60n2

Blavatsky, Helene, 117n3
body and mind, 71–72
body and soul, 162
Borg, Marcus, 81
Bosnia, 49
bounded-set groups, 158
Brown, Raymond E., 81
Brown, Robert, 78
Bucer, Martin, 57
Buda, 49
Buddha, 30
Buddhism, 96–97, 117n3
Bullinger, Heinrich, 57
Byzantine Empire, 48

cable of meaning, 34–38
Calvary Chapel, 156, 157
Calvary House, 92
Calvin, John, 20, 57
Campbell, Joseph, 67–70
capitalism, 51–52, 152
cash, 51–52
cell phones, 105
center-dwellers, 163n1
center-set-movement, 158–59
change, 114, 141
chaos math, 70
Charismatic Christians, 117n2, 126, 129
Christian exclusivity, 67, 69
church, as system of relations, 152
Civil Rights movement, 93
Civil War, 98–99
Clement VII, 44
clergy, authority of, 92–93
cognitive science, 71–72
Colet, John, 57
Columbus, 55
common imagination, 35
communism, 89–90
community, 151
community churches, 144n3
competition, over cooperation, 59
computer science, 70, 106–7
Conference of Conservative Protestants
    (1895), 65–66
Confucius, 30

consciousness, 73, 98
consensual illusion, 35, 45
Conservatives, 127, 154
Constantine, 161
Constantinople, 47–48
Contarini, Gasparo, 57
conversation, 104, 153
Copernicus, 54–55
Cordoba, 49
corporeality, 36–37, 39n1, 102
Council of Chalcedon, 23–24
Council of Trent, 58, 61n3
Counter-Emergence, 141
Counter-Reformation, 57–59, 61n3
creeds, 130
Crossan, John Dominic, 81
crowd sourcing, 152
Crusades, 59
culture, and religion, 33
cyberspace, 106–7

Dark Ages, 25–26, 151
Darwin, Charles, 54, 64–65, 73, 78
Darwinism, 55
de-Hellenization, 161, 162
democracy, 152, 153, 155
denominationalism, 46, 56, 101, 127–28
Descartes, René, 71–72, 74n1
dialectical materialism, 89
Diet of Speyer (1529), 124
divorce, 99–100, 112–13
doctrine, 102, 160, 161
drugs, 97–98, 125
Dyer, Mark, 16

earth, centrality of, 55–56
Eastern Orthodoxy, 20–21, 24, 28
economics, 15
egalitarianism, 84, 152
Eighty Years' War, 60
Einstein, Albert, 64, 77–82
electromagnetism, 64–65
electronic space, 106
Elnes, Eric, 142, 144n5
emergent, vs. emerging, 163n1

emergent Christianity, 28, 104, 116, 120, 121, 158. *See also* Great Emergence
empiricism, 54
Engels, Friedrich, 88
Enlightenment, 46, 90, 154
Episcopalians, 100, 130, 137
Erikson, Erik, 70
ethos, 34
evangelicalism, 144n3
  and Great Emergence, 153–54
evening services, 86
evolution, 54, 64, 65
experience, 93, 96

faith, and works, 56, 129
family, 87, 108–9, 112–15
Faraday, Michael, 64–65, 68, 73, 78
feminism, 109, 111
fiefdoms, 50, 151
Fifth Lateran Council, 57
flexibility, 154
folk wisdom, 90
form criticism, 81
Foster, Richard, 154
free time, 95
French Revolution, 88
Freud, Sigmund, 66–67, 70
Fuller Theological Seminary, 157
fundamentalism, 66, 127, 136

Galileo, 54
geriatric treatment, 105
globalization, 28, 52, 106
gnosticism, 161
God, as source of perfection, 150
Great Depression, 90, 95
Great Emergence, 13–16, 41–42
  and authority, 85, 145–46, 148, 150–53
  as conversation, 104, 153
  and evangelicalism, 153–54
  on humanness, 161–62
  as movement within Christianity, 120
  as postmodern, 159–60
  rewriting Christian theology, 162
Great Plague of Moscow, 60n2

Great Reformation, 19–20, 28, 42, 43–57, 120, 124, 151
Great Schism, 19–21, 27–28, 59
Great Society, 90
Greek Orthodoxy, 20–21, 24, 28
Greek philosophy, 161
Gregory the Great, 21–22, 25–26, 151
Gregory XII, 44
guilt, 42
gunpowder, 50
Gutenberg, Johannes, 52–54

Hegel, G. W. F., 88–89
Heisenberg Uncertainty Principle, 79, 81, 82, 116n1
Herzegovina, 49
hierarchy, 107, 108
Higher Power, 92–93
historical Jesus, 80–81
historicity, 149
HIV-AIDS, 60n2
Holy Spirit, 85, 146, 157
Homer, 30
homosexuality, 39n1, 101, 130, 137
Hooker, Richard, 20, 57
Hope Chapel, 156
Horney, Karen, 70
Hospitallers, 49
house church movement, 134
Hubble, Edwin, 82
humanness, 161–62
Hungary, 49
hyphenateds, 142–43

idealism, 54
Ignatius Loyola, 58
immigration, 93–95
incarnation, 23
incarnational churches, 135
independent churches, 143n3
individualism, 51, 152
indulgences, 58
inerrancy, 82
information, 15, 52, 106
inherited church, 136, 140, 141
Inquisition, 59

interdenominational churches, 144n3
Internet, 53, 70, 106, 135, 152
iPod, 105
Islam, 30, 47, 48, 49

James, William, 92
Jaspers, Karl, 30
Jesuits, 58
Jesus Christ, life, death, and resurrection, 26
Jesus scholarship, 81
Joachim of Fiore, 164n8
John Cassian, 27
John of the Cross, 58
John XXIII, 44
Jones, Tony, 163n1
Judaism, 29, 75n2, 120, 161
Jung, Carl, 67, 70

Keats, John, 150
Kepler, Johannes, 54
Kevorkian, Jack, 103, 105
Kimball, Dan, 163n1
King, Karen, 81
Knox, John, 20
Korean War, 94, 125

Lakewood Church (Houston), 144n3
Leary, Timothy, 98
Leo IX, 20
liberal theology, 65
light, 65
Lindley, David, 116n1
literacy, 28, 46, 151
literalism, 82
literary deconstruction, 79, 81
Liturgicals, 125–26, 128–29
logic, 160
Luther, Martin, 20, 43, 56, 124, 164n7

MacCulloch, Diarmaid, 60n1
Machiavelli, Niccolò, 54
machines, dependency on, 15
Marcian, 23
marriage, 112–15
Marx, Karl, 87–90

Mary, "Mother of God," 23–24
mathematics, 54
Maxwell, James Clerk, 68
McLaren, Brian, 163n1, 164n2, 164n7
McManus, Erwin, 163n1
meaning, 79
media age, 135
medical advances, 105
megachurch phenomenon, 144n3
Melanchthon, Philipp, 57
mercy, 103
meta-narrative, 160
Methodists, 127, 128
middle class, 51–52
Miller, Donald E., 155, 162, 164n3
modernism, 149
modernity, 136
monasticism, 22, 25–26, 27, 151
Monteverdi, 61n3
Moors, 49
morality, 36–37, 101–2
Mormons, 127
motion, 78
movement, 78
Moyers, Bill, 69
music, 53
Mussulmen, 48
mysticism, 159, 162, 164n8

Nag Hammadi, 81
nanotechnology, 70, 106
narrative, 160, 162
nation-states, 50, 51–52, 106
network theory, 70, 152–53, 154, 158
Neusner, Jacob, 81
New Deal, 90
new monasticism, 134
new paradigm churches, 155–56
Newton, Isaac, 54, 77
New World, 55–56
nondenominational churches, 134
North American Christianity, 121
nuclear family, 51–52, 108–9, 112

Oriental Christianity, 24, 27
orthodoxy, 131, 145, 147

orthonomy, 149–50, 163n1
orthopraxy, 130, 145, 147
Osiander, Andreas, 55
Ottomans, 47, 49
Oxford Group, 92

Pagels, Elaine, 81
Pagitt, Doug, 163n1, 164n6
Palmer, Parker, 154
pandemics, 60–61n2
Papacy, 104, 151
paper pope, 46
paradox, 160, 162
Parham, Charles, 83
particularity, Christian, 67, 69
Paul III, 58
Peace of Westphalia, 60
peasantry, 51
Pentecostalism, 82–85, 91, 126, 129, 158
peri-Reformation, 38, 47, 50, 52
physics, 64, 65
Planck, Max, 77
Plato, 30
Platonism, 54
political theory, 54, 88
post-Christendom, 136
post-Constantinianism, 161, 164n7
post-everything culture, 136
post-human theory, 70
postmodernity, 136, 141, 154
Power of Myth, The (PBS series), 69–70
pragmatism, 54
Presbyterians, 130, 137–38
priesthood of all believers, 45, 46, 53, 56, 107, 151, 155
Progressive Christians, 141–42
Protestantism, 17, 20, 28–29, 50–52, 56, 58, 87, 120, 159
  and authority, 101, 151
  divisiveness of, 46
  lacking a center, 134
  post-Emergence adaptations, 162–63
  shift away from, 143n3
psychology, 96
Publishers Weekly, 9–11
Purgatory, 58
purists, 138

quadrilateral illustration, 125–43, 145
Quakers, 127, 154–55, 157
quantum physics, 16, 77–78
Qumran, 81

radio, 68
Rank, Otto, 70
rationalism, 46
Rauschenbusch, Walter, 125, 142n1
reactionists, 138–39, 140, 144n4
realism, 54
reason, 90
re-formation, and authority, 45
Reformation. *See* Great Reformation
Reimarus, Hermann Samuel, 80, 81
relational, 153, 160
relativity, 78, 79, 82
religion, as social construct, 33
religion publishing, 9–11
religious enthusiasms, 21
Renaissance, 47–48
Renewalists, 117n2, 126, 146, 158
re-traditioning, 28, 58, 141, 142
revolution, 89
Rhodes, fall of, 49
Roe v. Wade, 102
Roman Catholicism, 17, 20, 27–29, 127–28, 159
  and counter-Reformation, 57–60
  in Great Emergence, 104
Roman Empire, death of, 22–23
rose symbol, 138
Rosie the Riveter, 108–11
rules, 158
rural life, 95, 132

Sabbath, 86–87
sacraments, 56
Schiavo, Terri, 103, 105
Schweitzer, Albert, 80–81
science, 54, 63–64
Scripture, authority of, 82, 151
Second Temple Judaism, 29
self, 70–72, 160, 162
seminaries, rise of, 58
serfdom, 50

Seymour, William, 82–83
Sheen, Fulton J., 68, 106
slavery, 98–99
small groups, 93
Smith, Bob, 91–92
Smith, Chuck, Jr., 156
Smith, Chuck, Sr., 156
Social Justice Christians, 126, 128–29, 137, 154
sociology, 11, 135, 155–56
Socrates, 30
sola scriptura, 45–46, 53, 56, 69, 80, 81, 137, 144n3, 146, 150
  erosion of, 98–101
  as outmoded and insufficient, 151
Solomon's Temple, 29
Sony Walkman, 105
soul, 78, 162
Southern Baptists, 127, 130
Spain, 48–49
spirituality, 36–37
Stalin, Joseph, 90
statism, 90
story, of community, 34, 52
Sunday, 86

technology, 15, 28, 64, 68, 86, 103–7
telegraph, 68
televangelists, 106
television, 68
Teresa of Ávila, 58
theonomy, 150, 163n1
Theosophy, 117n3
Third Wave, 157
Thirty Years' War, 59
Tillich, Paul, 125
tongues, 83, 158
tradition, 150
traditionalists, 140–41, 142
Treaty of Münster, 60
truth, 79
Twelve Steps, 92
two-income families, 114

unconscious, 66–67
Upanishads, 30
urbanization, 90, 95, 132
Urban VI, 44

Vatican I, 104–5
Vatican II, 104–5
Vespucci, Amerigo, 55
Vienna, 49
Vietnam War, 93, 94, 125
Vineyard movement. *See* Association of Vineyard Churches
Virgin birth, 149

Wagner, C. Peter, 157
warfare, 50, 59
watercooler theology, 132–34
Western Christianity, 24, 75n2
Willow Creek Church (South Barrington, Ill.), 144n3
Wilson, Bill, 91–92
Wimber, John, 155, 157–58
women
  enfranchisement of, 99
  equality of, 113
  ordination of, 100
  roles of, 87, 108–12
world, as flat, 15, 35–36, 55, 106
world exploration and trade, 28
world religions, 73
World War I, 95
World War II, 94, 108–11, 125
World Wide Web, 53, 70, 152
worship, 84, 155
Wright, N. T., 81
Wycliffe, John, 52

Zell, Matthias and Katharina, 57
Zwingli, Ulrich, 20, 57

Phyllis Tickle is founding editor of the Religion Department of *Publishers Weekly*. One of the most respected authorities and popular speakers on religion in America today, she is often quoted and interviewed in such media outlets as the *New York Times*, *USA Today*, *Newsweek*, *Time*, CNN, C-SPAN, and PBS. A lay eucharist minister in the Episcopal Church and a senior fellow of Cathedral College at the National Cathedral in Washington, she is the author of more than two dozen books, including *The Divine Hours* prayer manuals and, most recently, *The Words of Jesus: A Gospel of the Sayings of Our Lord*.